Launch into Literacy

Book 3

Jane Medwell
Maureen Lewis

OXFORD
UNIVERSITY PRESS

Contents

There is no time limit on the sessions and teachers will want to exercise their own skill and judgement when planning

 = whole class work

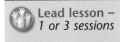
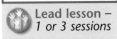

NLS planning chart

	Genre focus	Range of texts	Text features	Reading skills
UNIT·1	TERM 1 Writing to perform: playscripts	playscripts extract from a novel	stage directions and conventions of scripts dialogue script layout characterisation cast lists chronological order of events direct and reported speech	literal and inferential comprehension character analysis form action and dialogue comparing playscript and novel
UNIT·2	TERM 1 Writing to instruct: instructions on packets and packaging	seed packet plant food package	goal equipment steps to be taken lists	literal and inferential comprehension questions using a dictionary reading aloud to partner reading a chart 'reading' pictures
UNIT·3	TERM 2 Writing to express: classic narrative poem	extracts from 'The Pied Piper of Hamelin'	verses/verse structure rhyme repetition alliteration imagery metaphor similes	literal and inferential comprehension questions comparing characters using a dictionary reading aloud to partner
UNIT·4	TERM 2 Writing to inform: non-chronological reports	information book pages advertisement e-mail messages letters	hypothetical statements non-chronological order technical vocabulary headings passive sentences hypothetical statements	literal and inferential comprehension skimming
UNIT·5	TERM 3 Writing to entertain stories from other cultures	stories from another continent	characters setting plot events in order using dialogue	literal and inferential comprehension

Writing skills	Grammar	Punctuation	Words
writing summary notes chart completion writing direct speech as plays and prose writing reported speech time lines drafting a two scene play	adverbs	speech marks	idomatic expressions clichés

writing sentences
brainstorming ideas
planning an instructional
    package
drafting an instructional
    package
revising an instructional
    package
	auxiliary verbs
	main verbs
	verb mood
	adverbs
	adverbial phrases
	proper nouns
		colons
		bullet points
		commas
		semicolons
			definitions
			prefixes 'trans' and 'be'
			words ending in vowels

writing sentences
brainstorming ideas
planning a poem
drafting a poem
revising a poem
	main clauses
	subordinate clauses
	possessive pronouns
	possessive adjectives
	1st, 2nd and 3rd
	    person pronouns
		revision of apostrophes
		apostrophes of omission
		apostrophes of possession
		commas in complex
		    sentences
			rhyming words
			antonyms
			alliteration
			similes
			suffixes 'al' 'cian'

time line evaluating arguments note-making expanding and clarifying meaning writing a report	subject/verb agreement personal pronouns active and passive sentences possessive pronouns complex sentences connectives	replacing full stops with conjunctions	definitions technical words
brainstorming ideas planning a story drafting a story revising a story	adverbs punctuating dialogue conjunctions singular and plural forms apostrophe for possession complex sentences prepositions	commas	proverbs clichés

Writing to perform

In this unit you are going to study playscripts,
including ways they are set out and used.

The Lion, the Witch and the Wardrobe

Scene 2 The Steps of the Professor's House

brief description of the scene

Early evening in spring. The FOUR *children walking towards the steps leading up to a rambling country house.*

Out of the house comes the Housekeeper, MRS MACREADY.

MACREADY:	So! You'll be the Evacuees.
LUCY:	We're the Pevensies.
MACREADY:	How nice for you! Ration books, if you please! [*The* FOUR *children proffer ration books.*] One, two, three, four. Well, I suppose we'll find room for you.
PROFESSOR:	[*Appearing on the top step.*] Of course we will. We'll find a couple of rooms for them. Let me see, [*Descending and shaking hands with each in turn.*] – you will be Peter. And Susan. Edgar.
EDMUND:	No, Edmund.
PROFESSOR:	I beg your pardon – Edmund. And Lucy, child of light.
LUCY:	Just Lucy, sir.
PROFESSOR:	I'm Professor Kirk – this is my house and behold, this is my housekeeper, Mrs Macready. I find it wise to obey her in most things. I hope your stay here will be happy and exciting.
PETER:	Thank you, sir.
PROFESSOR:	I'm off to hide in my study and work. So I will say good night.
THE FOUR:	Good night, sir.
PROFESSOR:	Mrs Macready will show you to your rooms.
MACREADY:	This way children!

information about what character does while speaking

The names of the speakers are on the left hand side of the page

PETER, SUSAN, EDMUND *and* LUCY *follow* MACREADY *out.*

Scene 3 The Girls' Bedroom

Enter MACREADY, *followed by the* FOUR *with their cases.*

The room is light, with a big arched window. There are bookcases, with plenty of old books. On top of the bookcases are glass cases with various stuffed birds, fish and small mammals. Also two brass beds, with patchwork quilts.

Playscripts

- What clues suggest that this is near the beginning of the play?
- What would the stage set for this scene look like?
- How do you imagine the Professor's appearance?
- Why is the dialogue set out like this?

UNIT·1 **Writing to perform**

Text features:
*dialogue,
stage directions,
information about
the characters,
clues to the plot*

*information about
what happens on stage*

MACREADY:	The young ladies will sleep in here.
LUCY:	And the young gentlemen?
MACREADY:	Through the blue door and mind your heads. You'll find the necessaries under your beds. Good night, sleep tight, mind the beasties don't bite.
THE FOUR:	Good night!

Exit MACREADY. *The* FOUR *try bouncing on beds.*

PETER:	We've fallen on our feet and no mistake. The Professor will let us do what we like.
SUSAN:	He's an old dear.
EDMUND:	[*Tapping the glass case of a stuffed badger.*] Oh, come off it! Don't talk like that.
SUSAN:	Like what?
EDMUND:	Like Mother.
SUSAN:	Edmund, it's time you were in bed.
EDMUND:	There you are. Go to bed yourself, Susan.
PETER:	[*Changing the subject.*] This whole house is like the maze at Hampton Court.
EDMUND:	That was hedges, not rooms.
LUCY:	What's that noise?
EDMUND:	Only a bird, silly.
LUCY:	It makes me feel creepy.
PETER:	It's an owl. This is going to be a wonderful place for birds. [*Stretching.*] I'm off to bed. We can explore tomorrow. You saw those mountains and woods? There might be eagles.
SUSAN:	Stags, perhaps.
PETER:	It'll be dragons and serpents if we don't get to bed. Come on Edmund. Good night, girls!
THE FOUR:	Good night!
SUSAN:	[*Using their Mother's formula.*] Happy dreams.

Exit PETER *and* EDMUND *through the blue door.*

from *The Lion, the Witch and the Wardrobe* by C. S. Lewis

*The names of the speakers are
the left hand side of the page*

*The words spoken by the characters
are written without speech marks*

Remember

Try to imagine how the play would look when acted out.

Comprehension

1 Reread the extract on pages 4 and 5.

2 Now answer these questions.
   a The children are at the Professor's house
   because he is their grandfather?
   because they are evacuees?
   because they have nowhere else to go?
   b Mrs Macready is
   the housekeeper?
   a teacher for the children?
   a visitor in the house?
   c The children in the play
   already know the Professor?
   know about him but have not met him before?
   have never heard of the Professor?
   d The children call the Professor 'sir' because
   he is a knight?
   he is older than they are?
   he is their teacher?

3 In which decade do you think the play is set?

4 Reread the two brief scene descriptions. These tell us something about the Professor. Use the evidence to collect information about the Professor.

5 Why do you think Peter is sure the Professor will let them do as they want. Write what you think and why.

Glossary
playscript

6

Studying characters

At the beginning of a play there is usually a **cast list**. This is a list of the **characters** in the play, with a few words of description about each character.

1 Reread the extract from *The Lion, the Witch and the Wardrobe* on pages 4 and 5. Make a list of the characters and give a very brief description of each character.

> Cast list
> Peter   The eldest boy. Polite.
> Susan

In plays there are a number of ways to decide what a character is like:

- Listen to what the character says to other characters.
- See what the character does.
- Observe how other characters talk and act towards the character.

2 What do you think Peter is like? Explain why you would or would not like him if you met him in real life.

3 Collect evidence about the characters in the playscript and complete a chart like the one below.

	What he/she says to other characters	What he/she does	How other characters talk and act towards him/her
Mrs Macready			The Professor suggests she has to be obeyed. The children are polite.
The Professor	Is polite to everyone. Introduces himself to the children and welcomes them.		
Edmund	He's argumentative with Peter and Susan. Unkind to Lucy.		

4 Now write a short character sketch about each of the characters in the chart, based on your evidence.

> Glossary
> character

Dialogue

Dialogue is written speech, when two or more **characters** are speaking. In playscripts this is set out so that the actors can read it easily.

EXAMPLE:

The actual words spoken

SAM : **I'm starving.**
MUM : **Here's your dinner, then.**

The character speaking

A new line for each speaker

1 Rewrite the speech bubbles as a playscript.

Sometimes authors put **stage directions** into the character's speech so the actor will know how to say something.
EXAMPLE: **EDMUND:** [*rudely*] I don't know.

2 Choose two different **adverbs** which could go into the stage directions for each sentence below. The first one is done for you.

a SALLY: [*loudly*] Please help me!
   SALLY: [*weakly*] Please help me!
b FARMER BIGGS: [   ] Don't climb over that gate!
c PC JONES: [   ] Well, well, well! And what have we got here then?
d JOE: [   ] I'm sorry I'm late. Really sorry.
e MISS TODE: [   ] Do get your PE clothes on, please.

The conventions of scripts

A **playscript** tells the actors what to do using stage directions. This helps them to act the play out and create the scenes.

EXAMPLE: *Out of the house comes the Housekeeper, Mrs Macready*

1 Reread the passage from *The Lion, the Witch and the Wardrobe* on pages 4 and 5. Make notes of all the stage directions.

2 Using your notes, finish the **time line** (or flow chart) below, which shows the order of the actions in this part of the play. You can put in any extra detail that you imagine will fit the script.

> The children are walking up to a rambling country house.

> Mrs Macready, the housekeeper, comes out of the house.

3 Write brief notes of what the **characters** say next to your timeline.

Other stage directions which are included in a line of speech tell the actor what the character is doing as he or she speaks.

EXAMPLE: **EDMUND:** [*Tapping the glass case of a stuffed badger*]
Oh, come off it!

4 Rewrite this piece of dialogue. Fill in the stage directions with the actions the characters are doing.

JANE: [   ] Arrgh! Ooooh! Ah! Ow!

ANDREW: [   ] It wasn't my fault.

JANE: [   ] Yes it was. You dropped the TV on my foot. I bet you've broken it.

MUM: [   ] What's going on here?

ANDREW:
JANE: } [   ] Nothing.

Glossary

playscript
time line
character

9

Characters in a story and a play

Read this extract from the play of
Charlie and the Chocolate Factory by Roald Dahl.

WILLY WONKA:	Welcome! Welcome! Welcome! Hello, everyone! Let's see now. I wonder if I can recognize all of you by the pictures of you in the newspaper. Let's see [*Pause*] You're Augustus Gloop.
AUGUSTUS GLOOP:	Uhhhh … y-e-a-hhhh and this is … uhh … my mother.
WILLY WONKA:	Delighted to meet you both! Delighted! Delighted! [*Turns to Violet*] You're Violet Beauregarde.
VIOLET BEAUREGARDE:	So what if I am – let's just get on with the whole thing, huh?
WILLY WONKA:	And you must be Mrs Beauregarde. Very happy to meet you! Very happy! [*Turns to Veruca*] I think you are … yes … you're Veruca Salt. And you must be Mr and Mrs Salt.
VERUCA SALT:	Don't shake his hand, Daddy – it's probably all sticky and chocolatey from working in the factory. After all, he *does* only run a silly little factory. He's not important enough for you to bother shaking hands with, anyway!
WILLY WONKA:	You're Mike Teavee. Enchanted to meet you!
MR AND MRS TEAVEE:	And we're the Teavees. Pleased to meet you.
WILLY WONKA:	Overjoyed! Overjoyed! [*Turns to Charlie*] And you must be the boy who just found the ticket yesterday. Congratulations! You're … Charlie Bucket – aren't you?
CHARLIE:	Yes sir, thank you. And this, sir, is my Grandpa Joe.

1 Draw a table like the one below. For each character make a note of what they say in Column A. Use this to draw a conclusion about what each character is like, writing this in Column B.

| Character | Column A | Column B
Evidence deduction | Column C
Physical description |
|---|---|---|---|
| Willy Wonka | Very happy
Enchanted
Overjoyed | | Voice high and flutey |
Augustus Gloop			
Charlie Bucket			
Veruca Salt			

UNIT·1 **Writing
to perform**

Text features:
setting
Reading skills:
comprehension

2 Write a full **cast list** for this
scene of the play, with a few
words about each **character**

Cast list
Willy Wonka - very excited, friendly

Compare the passage on page 10 with this passage from the
novel *Charlie and the Chocolate Factory* by Roald Dahl.

Will you come forward one at a time, please,' he called out, 'and bring
your parents. Then show me your Golden Ticket and give me your
name. Who's first?'

The big fat boy stepped up. 'I'm Augustus Gloop,' he said.

'Augustus!' cried Mr Wonka, seizing his hand and pumping up and
down with terrific force.

'My *dear* boy, how *good* to see you! Delighted! Charmed! Overjoyed to
have you with us! And *these* are your parents? How *nice*! Come in!
Come in! That's right! Step through the gates!'

Mr Wonka was clearly just as excited as everybody else.

'My name,' said the next child to go forward, 'is Veruca Salt.'

'My *dear* Veruca! How *do* you do? What a pleasure this is! You *do*
have an interesting name, don't you? I always thought that a veruca was
a sort of wart that you got on the sole of your foot! But I must have
been wrong, mustn't I? How pretty you look in that lovely mink coat!
I'm so glad you could come! Dear me, this is going to be *such* an
exciting day! I *do* hope you enjoy it! I'm sure you *will*! I *know* you will!
Your father? How *are* you, Mr Salt? And Mrs Salt? Overjoyed to see
you! Yes, the ticket is quite in order! Please go in!'

The next two children, Violet Beauregarde and Mike Teavee, came
forward to have their tickets examined and then to have their arms
practically ripped off their shoulders by the energetic Mr Wonka.

And last of all, a small nervous voice whispered, 'I'm Charlie Bucket.'

'Charlie!' cried Mr Wonka. 'Well, well, well! So there you are! You're
the one who found your ticket only yesterday, aren't you? Yes, yes. I
read *all* about it in this morning's papers! *Just* in time, my dear boy! I'm
so glad! So happy for you!'

3 List three ways in which this passage is different from the play.

4 List three ways in which this passage is similar to the play.

5 The story is told by a **narrator** who tells the reader what the
characters say and what they look like and do. Fill in some
information about what the characters look and sound like
the one on page 10.

6 Write a time line to show what Willy Wonka does.

Glossary
cast list
character
novel
narrator

Remember

Use speech marks around what is actually said, including the punctuation.

Remember

Start a new line for each person who speaks.

Direct and reported speech

In a story we are told what the characters say. When the actual words are given as if they were spoken this is called **direct speech**. When the narrator tells us what someone said we call it **reported speech**.

EXAMPLE: "Help, help!" screamed Joe. (direct speech)

Joe screamed for help again and again.
(reported speech)

1 Change these passages of reported speech into direct speech.
   a The waiter asked if I wanted anything to eat, so I said I would have a cheese sandwich.
   b Charlie said that he wanted to go to the park, but Liam replied that he would rather go to the swimming pool. In the end, Charlie agreed to go to the pool.
   c Mum asked what I did at school today. I told her that I just did what I usually did. Then she moaned that I never tell her anything.

Sometimes direct speech is broken up in a sentence using commas.

EXAMPLE: "My name," said the next child to go forward, "is Veruca Salt."

2 Write these sentences out, adding speech marks and commas.
   EXAMPLE: I'm sorry I said it wasn't me.
      "I'm sorry," I said, "it wasn't me."
   a This book moaned Rajiv is really awful.
   b Hello shouted the girl is there anybody there?
   c Of course said the teacher you must be the new boy.
   d It is so delicious mumbled Janice through a mouthful of cake that I will have another slice.

Glossary

speech marks

UNIT·1 Writing
to perform

Text features:
playscripts
Grammar:
direct speech

Direct speech in stories and scripts

There are two main ways of writing **direct speech**. In stories **speech marks** are used. In plays the speech is set out as a script.

commas where the direct speech is broken up

"Oh no," said Goldilocks, "I can hear someone coming."
"Hello, hello," shouted a voice, "who's been sitting in my chair?"

a new line for each speaker

stage directions

verbs in the past tense

GOLDILOCKS: Oh no [*looks around for a place to hide*] I can hear someone coming!

BEAR: Hello, hello, who's been sitting in my chair?

name of speaker

GRANGE HILL

1 School entrance
[Benny Green is bouncing his football off the wall. He steps into the path of an oncoming car… The car just manages to stop.]

MR MITCHELL: What do you think you are doing playing in the car park?! I could have easily killed you then!

BENNY: Yes sir, but I was …

MR MITCHELL: I know what you were doing. You were too involved with that football! Benny Green, isn't it? [*Benny, still a little shaken, can only nod his head*] You played for your last school team, didn't you? [*Benny nods again*] Going to try for the team here? The trials are tonight, you know.

BENNY: Yes sir, you told us yesterday.

MR MITCHELL: Have you brought your kit?

BENNY: I've got my PE kit, sir.

MR MITCHELL: No boots?

BENNY: Haven't got any, sir. The ones I had are too small and my dad gave them to my brother.

MR MITCHELL: Well, I don't think you'll be allowed to … still, we'll see. [*Benny starts to go*] And Green … watch where you're going in future. My nerves won't stand another incident like that. [*Benny manages a smile and walks away*]

Remember

Use past tense verbs like 'said', 'whispered' etc.

1 Finish writing this part of the playscript of *Grange Hill* as direct speech in a story.

"Benny Green, isn't it?" asked Mr Mitchell. "You played for your school team, didn't you? Going to try for the team here? The trials are tonight, you know," he continued.
"Yes, sir, you told us yesterday," replied Benny.

Glossary
direct speech
speech marks
past tense
verb

13

Studying a script

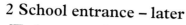

1 Read this second extract from *Grange Hill*.

2 School entrance – later

[Tucker enters the gate, hands in pockets, tie hanging loosely. He spots his two friends – Alan and David – runs up and jumps on their shoulders, causing them all to fall in a heap. Tucker's bag opens – the contents spill out. As they sort themselves out they turn and find Mr Foster, a PE teacher, towering over them.

MR FOSTER: *[to Tucker]* Fancy yourself as something of a circus performer, do you son? A bit of a clown, are you? What would your mother say if she saw you rolling about in those new clothes?

TUCKER: Don't know, sir.

MR FOSTER: Oh, I'm sure you do son. She'd more than likely box your ears. What's your name?

TUCKER: Er …

MR FOSTER: I can't hear you son. Get some air into your lungs.

TUCKER: Jenkins sir!

MR FOSTER: Jenkins? Do I know you?

TUCKER: Don't think so, sir.

MR FOSTER: Didn't I have to speak to you on your first day? In the Main Hall?

TUCKER: *[innocent]* No sir. Not me sir.

MR FOSTER: Don't mess me about son. It doesn't pay.

TUCKER: It wasn't me sir.

MR FOSTER: Hhhhhmmmmmm. Well I'll be watching out for you Jenkins. Remember that. Now clear off before you really do something to upset me. And don't let me catch you acting the buffoon again.

Remember
Reported speech does not use the words actually spoken or speech marks.

2 What were the children doing as the teacher arrived?

3 Write a **stage direction** to say what the boys do when they see the teacher arrive.

4 Why does Tucker say that his name is Jenkins?

5 Describe how the boys felt as they walked away.

6 Complete this account of what happened in the play, using **reported speech**

Glossary
stage direction
reported speech

Mr Foster asked Tucker what his name was. Tucker hesitated, so Mr Foster asked him to speak up. Quickly, Tucker said…

Idiomatic expressions

Idiomatic expressions are sentences or phrases that cannot be understood just by reading the words. They are understood by the group of people who use them.

EXAMPLES: 'Under the weather' means not feeling too well.
'Over the moon' means feeling delighted about something.

1 Read the *Grange Hill* extract on page 14 carefully and work out definitions for these idiomatic expressions.
   a "box your ears"
   b "mess me about"
   c "Get some air into your lungs."
   d "clear off"
   e "acting the buffoon"

Idiomatic expressions are very common in **dialogue**. Some expressions are used so often that they become repetitive or boring. We call such expressions **clichés.**

2 Here are some clichés. Write out definitions to explain what each one means.
   a As sick as a parrot.
   b Rome wasn't built in a day.
   c At this moment in time.
   d A stitch in time saves nine.

3 Rewrite the boy's speech, right, replacing the clichés with your own expressions.

Well, I must say, that was a tiring walk. I'm dead on my feet and I can't walk another step. Mum usually collects me from school dead on time; she's as regular as clockwork. I don't know why she didn't arrive. Maybe something's come up.

Glossary
dialogue

Writing a playscript

You are going to write a playscript for a play of
two short scenes, suitable for children to perform.
Here are some ideas for what might
happen in the play.

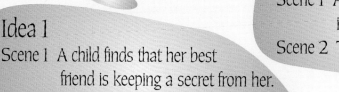

Idea 2
Scene 1 A child gets an
              invitation to a tea party.
Scene 2 The tea party is a disaster.

Idea 1
Scene 1 A child finds that her best
              friend is keeping a secret from her.
Scene 2 She follows her friend and finds
              her friend has planned a surprise party.

Discuss

1 Choose which idea you will develop into a short play.

2 Discuss the idea with a partner and brainstorm some ideas.
Make sure your play is very short, because dialogue takes up
a great deal of space.

3 Write a time line of what will happen in your play.

Most things must happen through what people say.

Sarah talks to her friend Mae.
Mae keeps laughing
and won't say why.

Sarah goes off in a sulk.

Plan

4 Think about your main character and make notes about:
- the character's name.
- the character's appearance
- the character's personality
- the way the character talks.

You will need to show what the character is like
through their words.

5 Decide on one or two other characters who will be in the play. Write a full cast list with a few words of description about each character.

> Cast list
> Aunt Flo   – an elderly, deaf relation sitting at breakfast.
> Benzny   – an energetic boy whose aunt doesn't understand him.

6 Decide on a simple setting for each scene of the play.
Where will each scene of the play take place?
Will the scene take place during the day or at night?
What sort of furniture will you need to have for each scene?

7 Write a short scene description for each scene.

8 Now write the dialogue for each scene – exactly what each character says.

The words spoken by the actors

The speaker's name on the left hand side

> SARAH: Go on Mitra. Tell me, please?
> MITRA: [Turning her face away] Nope. Sorry.
> SARAH: That's so mean. Really mean.
> MITRA: Sorry!

A new line for each speaker

short, clear sentences which sound natural

stage directions to say what the actors should do

Draft

9 Now write out a second draft of your play. Make sure it includes:
- a cast list
- a scene description for each scene
- dialogue that is clearly set out.

Revise

10 Read the play with a friend and discuss it using the following questions.
- Is it clear what happens in the play?
- Does the play have a good ending?
- Does the way the characters talk show what they are like?
- Do the stage directions tell you what to do?

11 Make whatever changes are needed to improve your play.

12 Present your play to a group of children in your class.

Publish

Writing to instruct

Instructions tell us how to do or make something. In this unit you will study how instructions are written. You will also see how they are sometimes just a part of a longer text. At the end of the unit you will plan, draft and write a set of instructions.

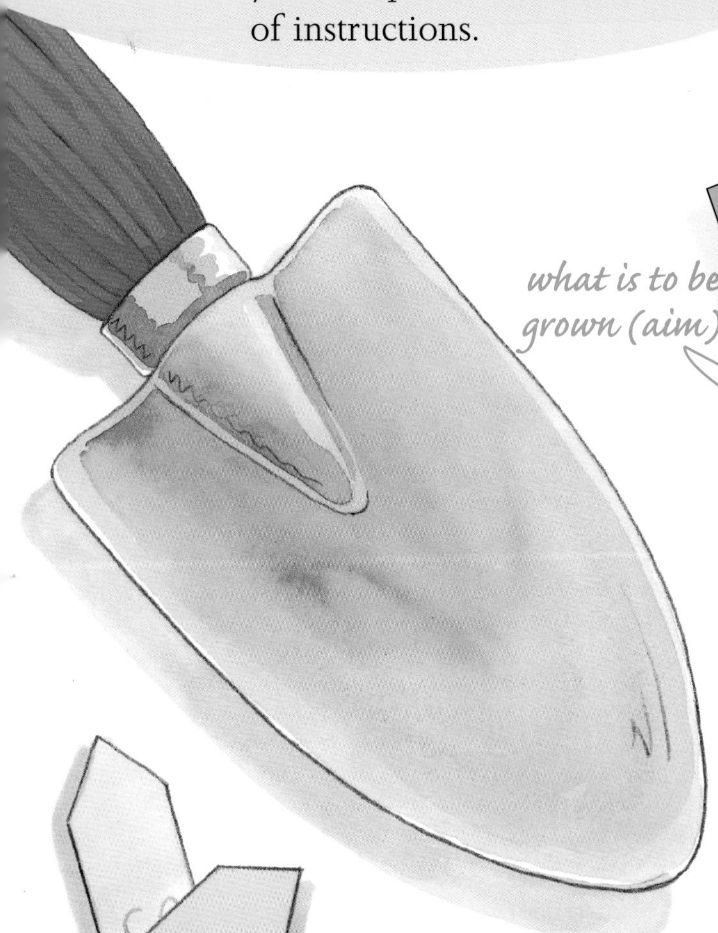

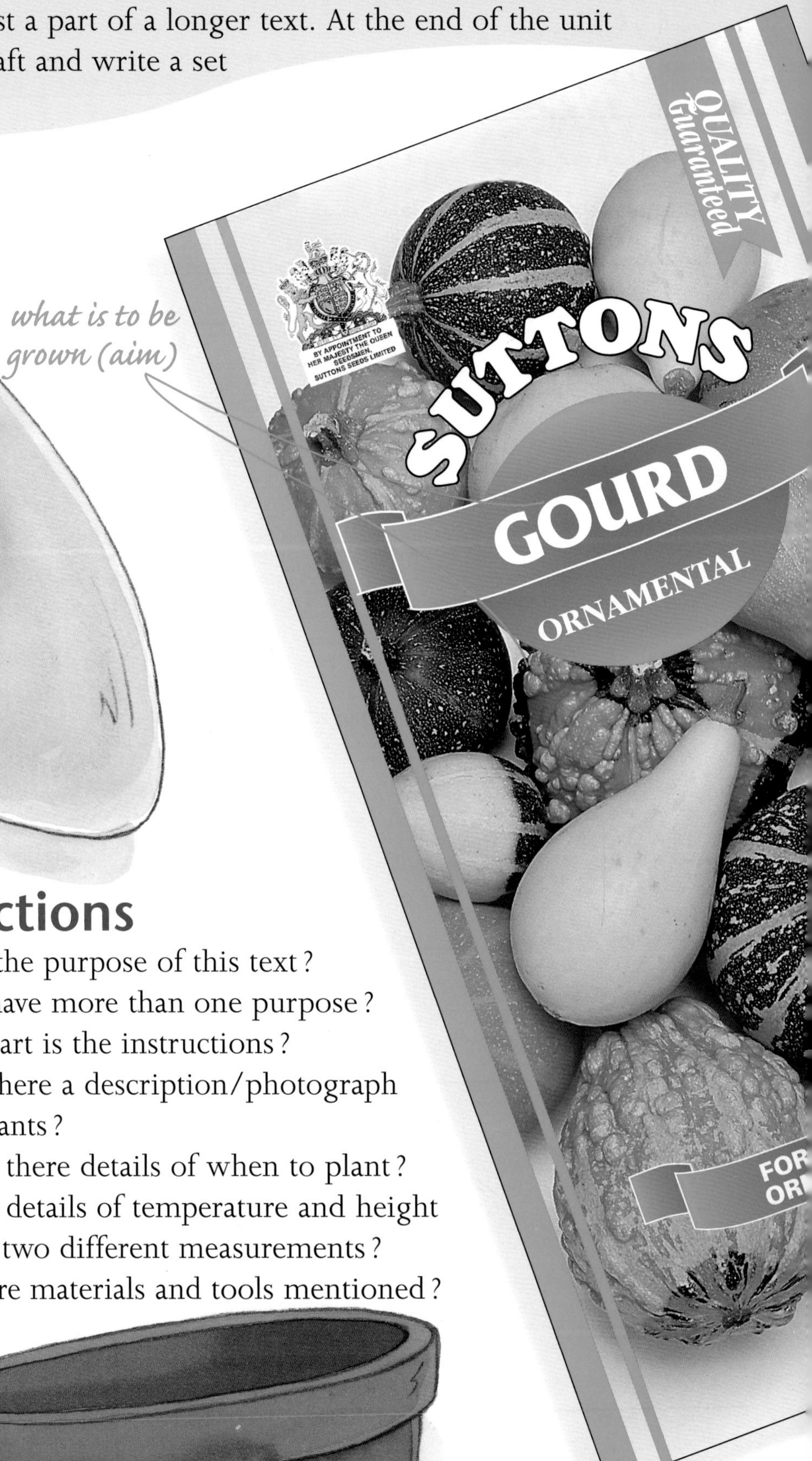

what is to be grown (aim)
QUALITY Guaranteed
BY APPOINTMENT TO HER MAJESTY THE QUEEN SEEDSMEN, SUTTONS SEEDS LIMITED
SUTTONS
GOURD
ORNAMENTAL

parsley

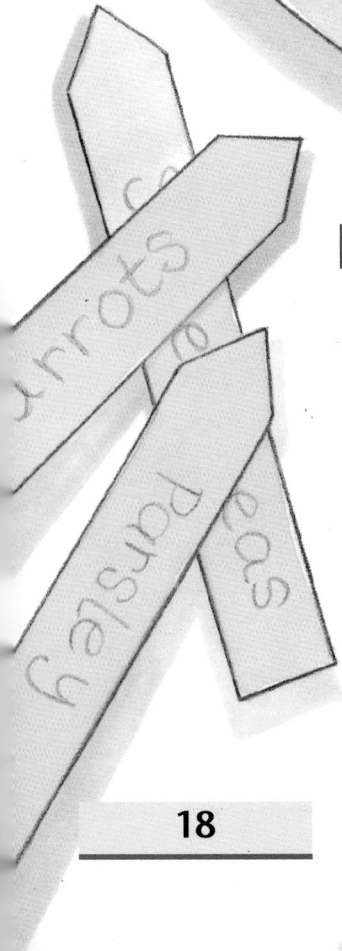

Instructions

- What is the purpose of this text? Does it have more than one purpose?
- Which part is the instructions?
- Why is there a description/photograph of the plants?
- Why are there details of when to plant?
- Why are details of temperature and height given in two different measurements?
- Where are materials and tools mentioned?

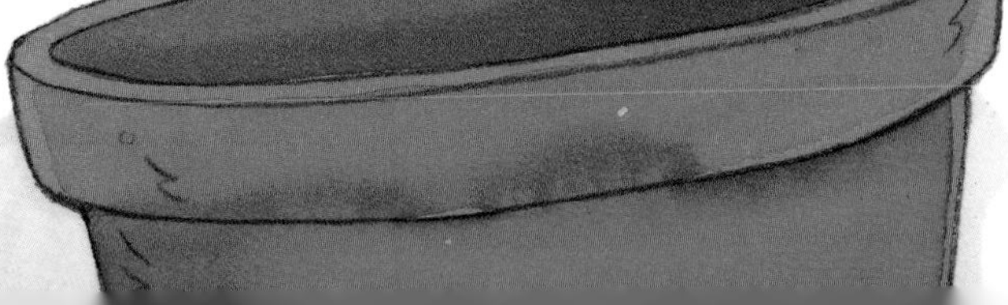

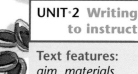

abbreviations

sales details

Ave. seed content 20
Sow by 1/200
        D

99p

GOURD
ORNAMENTAL (Not Edible)
Grow as a Half Hardy Annual (Sow under cover)

13 68 66

 SOW

 PLANTING OUT

 FLOWERING/ HARVEST

instructions in graphic form

JAN	FEB	MAR	APR	MAY	JUN	JUL	AUG	SEP	OCT	NOV	DEC

DESCRIPTION: Plants resemble trailing marrows and produce small, hard fruits in many unusual shapes and colours. The fruits are very effective for indoor decoration.

SOWING/GROWING: Sow in a propagator on a window-sill or in a greenhouse, at approx. 18–21°C (65–70°F) using a good quality, moist compost. Cover the seeds with 19 mm (3/4 in.) sieved compost. Transplant seedlings singly into 75 mm (3 in.) pots and grow on. Acclimatize plants gradually before planting out 90–120 cm (3 ft–4 ft.) apart in an open sunny position. Will ramble over the ground or may be trained up trellis and fences, etc.

instructions

precise details

specialist vocabulary

adverbs

HELPFUL HINT: After careful drying, fruits can be waxed or varnished for table decoration.

QUALITY CONTROL
The seed in this packet has been carefully processed to ensure good germination and the development of strong, healthy seedlings. Until required for use, the seed should be stored in a cool dry place.

9 780199 147410

SUTTON SEEDS LTD TORQUAY ENGLAND

sales details

Comprehension and vocabulary

1 Look again at the seed packet on page 19. Answer these questions about the packet.

   a Which company is selling these seeds?

   b How much does the packet cost and how many seeds does it contain?

   c What can the fruits of the plant be used for? What can they not be used for?

   d What are the seeds covered with when they are first planted?

   e In what kind of place is it best to plant the seedlings?

   f Why do you think there is a 'sow by' date on the packet?

2 What do these words from the packet mean?
Write a **definition** for each one.

   a annual

   b edible

   c effective

   d sieved

   e compost

   f acclimatize

   g germination

Remember
You can use a dictionary to look up word meanings.

3 The equipment you need to plant the seeds is not listed separately on the packet because different things are needed at different times. Copy the following headings and fill in the lists, using the text, the pictures and the chart to help you.

In April you need: In June you need:

Lists, colons and bullet points

1 Look at question 3 on page 20. Did you create a list like this?

> In April you need:
> • seeds,
> • sieved compost,
> • moist compost,
> • a propagator.

The list has been punctuated using a **colon** (:), **bullet points** (•), **commas** (,)and a *full stop*. The colon marks the start of the list, the bullet points draw attention to each item in the list, the commas separate items in a list, and the full stop marks the end.

Remember
Some lists do not have bullet points, and others use commas and bullet points.

2 Find examples of printed lists in books, newspapers and magazines. Examine how they have been punctuated.

3 Change the following sentence lists into bullet-pointed lists. Add colons, bullet points and full stops. Drop any words you do not need.
   a The garden shed contains tools, plant pots, compost, fertilizer, bulbs and seeds.
   b The hanging basket included lobelia, fuschia, nasturtiums, ivy and trailing geraniums.
   c For a trek on Dartmoor you will need a map, compass, torch, emergency rations, whistle or mobile phone, waterproof clothing, jumper, gloves, a scarf and high factor sun-cream.

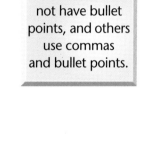

4 Make a list of the items you would pack for a weekend staying at a hotel with a swimming pool.

Glossary
full stop

Main verbs and auxiliary verbs

> **HELPFUL HINT:** After careful drying, fruits can be waxed or varnished for table decoration.

'Can be varnished' is a **verb** phrase which is made up of a **main verb** ('varnish') and two **auxiliary verbs** ('can', 'be').

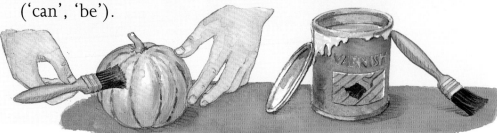

1 Circle the main verbs in these sentences. Underline the auxiliary verbs. The first one is done for you.

    a He was planting the seeds.

       He <u>was</u> (planting) the seeds.

    b Sun can shine on the seeds.

    c Rain will water the seeds.

    d The plant grows very tall.

    e We must eat lots of fruit and vegetables.

2 Here are the chief, modal auxiliary verbs.

can   may   will   shall   must
could   might   would   should

3 Complete these sentences by adding an ending that includes a main verb.

    a He could …   **b** They might …

    c The cats would …   **d** Gardeners should …

    e We must …   **f** Plants can …

    g Teachers may …   **h** It will …

    i I shall …

Glossary
verb

More about auxiliary verbs

There are three verbs that can be either **auxiliary verbs** or **main verbs**. They are the verbs: 'to be', 'to have', 'to do'.
Used as a main verb:
EXAMPLES: He **is** good. She **has** a cat. They **did** well.
Used as an auxiliary verb:
EXAMPLES: He **is running**. She **has eaten** it.
They **do like** sweets.

Remember
The verb 'to be' changes: I am, he/she is, you/we/they are, I/he/she was, you/we/they were. The verbs 'to have' and 'to do' also change.

1 Decide whether the verbs 'to be', 'to have' and 'to do' are being used as a main verb or an auxiliary verb in the following **sentences**. Write 'main' or 'auxiliary'.

  a They are enjoying the film.

  b She does not smoke.

  c He is a big man.

  d The toddler has lost his mum.

  e They are hot and thirsty.

  f The plants have grown well.

'Not' can be inserted between the auxiliary verb and the main verb. EXAMPLE: The seeds **should not be stored**.
'Not' is not used when a main verb has no auxiliary with it.
EXAMPLE: He runs not. ✗
We usually add an auxiliary verb if we wish to change the sentence to a negative form.
EXAMPLE: She jumps. She **does not jump**.

Remember
'Not' can be shortened to n't when it goes with an auxiliary verb: have n't, is n't, does n't.

2 Change these sentences into negatives by inserting 'not'. You might also need to add an auxiliary verb.

  a She has arrived.

  b The plants grow bigger and bigger.

  c I shall water them every day.

  d I will pick the fruit.

  e We eat the fruit for lunch.

  f We might give some to you.

3 Look at the sentences you have just written. Write the shortened form of the auxiliary + not alongside each sentence.

Glossary
auxiliary verb
main verb
sentence

Adding detail to the verb

An **adverb** is a single word that tells us how, when or where the verb happens.

EXAMPLE: Transplant (verb) the seedlings singly.
(adverb – how)

An **adverbial phrase** is made from linked words that tells us how, when or where the verb happens.

EXAMPLE: We will walk over the hills.
(adverbial phrase – where)

1 Copy this passage. Put a circle round the adverbs and underline the adverbial phrases.

Sunflowers grow quickly. They like to be planted in a sunny spot. Be sure to water them frequently as they need lots of water. If you dry the flower heads carefully you can use the seeds. They can be used to plant again next year or you could feed them to the birds. You will see the birds greedily eating the seeds.

2 Here is a boring newspaper report about a gardener. Write it out adding your own choice of adverbs or adverbial phrases.

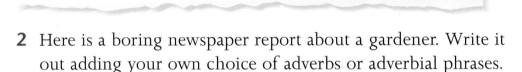

Lady Ploomstead nearly hit by her gardener

When? Mr Jones, the gardener at Ploomstead Manor was working *where?* Some one was moving *how?* outside the door. *How?* Mr Jones moved to the door. He could hear the sound of footsteps *where?* .

"I thought no one was in but me. We had two antique statues stolen *when?*," said Mr Jones. "So I picked up a spade and leapt (*how?*) outside. I felt *how?* when I saw it was Her Ladyship. *How?* I stopped *when?* Her Ladyship laughed *how?* at my mistake, but next time I'll be more careful."

Adding prefixes

The seed packet on page 19 says "Transplant the seedlings".
'Transplant' is made from adding the **prefix** 'trans-' to the
root word '-plant'.

1 'Trans-' often means to move or change from one person,
place or state to another. This can help you work out the
meaning. Say what the following words means.
   a transcribe   **b** transatlantic
   c transform   **d** transfusion

Remember
You can check
your definition
in a dictionary.

2 Make your own list of words that begin with the prefix
'trans-'. Compare your list with a partner's.

3 One important prefix that comes from old English is 'be-'.
Make a list of words by adding the prefix 'be-' to these base
words. **come** have **hold** hind
half tween. fore side

4 Now add some more words of your own to your list.

You can change a noun into a verb by adding the prefix 'be-'.
EXAMPLES: be + wail = bewail   be + siege = besiege
The verb then means to make, do or become something
to do with the base word.

5 Change these nouns into verbs by using the prefix 'be-'.

rate troth **moan** muse

6 Draw a picture of a besuited man and
a beribboned lady getting betrothed.

7 Complete the sentence
"They are getting betrothed
because…" using as many 'be-'
words as you can.

Glossary
definition

25

More instructions

Now we are going to look at another package which contains instructions. It is the front and back of a package of plant food. Again the instructions are only part of the text.

what is to be achieved (aim)

instructions

specialist vocabulary

some details given in graphic form

precise details

Plant Food

Balanced to work in four ways: Nitrogen promotes healthy foliage, Potash develops abundant flowers & fruit, Phosphate develops a strong root system. Essential Trace Elements keep plants healthy.

What plants can be fed & when

• All types of plant, both outside and indoors, use Plant Food regularly throughout the growing season.

How to use feed

1 With a watering can dilute with water as shown in the chart below.
2 Apply Plant Food solution around roots of plants.
3 Also apply Plant Food solution to foliage, for foliar feeding, but never foliar feed in direct sunlight.
• Alternatively, to effectively feed and water your garden in minutes use a Phostrogen Handy Feeder, Easy Feeder or Thru' Hose Feeder. Simply pour the enclosed 250 g sachet of feed into the feeder bowl and use as directed in feeder instructions.

How much and how often

Plants to be fed	Watering Can	Phostrogen Feeders	Feeding Frequency
General Garden Flowers, shrubs, trees, lawns, fruit & vegetables	4 teaspoons per 10 litres (2 gallons) water	250 g sachet per fill	7–14 days
Container and Young Plants and Seedlings	1 teaspoon per 10 litres	250 g sachet per fill	At every watering
Tomatoes	4 teaspoons per 10 litres	– – – – – –	7 days after first flowers have set
House Plants	3 pinches per 1 litre	– – – – – –	At every watering

! What else to know

• Safe for children and pets (except fish).
• Pour any unused solution onto bare soil not grass.
• Any spillage of concentrate or powder onto lawns or foliage should be thoroughly watered in immediately.

adverbs

UNIT·2 Writing to instruct

Text features:
*instructions,
grammar, verbs,
adverbs,
vocabulary,
definitions*

Some of this text gives instructions. Some of it tries to persuade you to buy the packet.

1 Look carefully at the packet and then answer these questions.
  a What four things does the plant food do?
  b How often should you feed general garden plants?
  c How much plant food do you need to mix if you are going to feed tomato plants?
  d Which two parts of a plant can you apply the feed to?
  e Why do you think the picture shows a healthy, colourful garden?
  f Why do you think the picture shows a child and a dog playing in the garden?
  g Why do you think the packet says it is 'easy to use'?

2 Give a definition for the following words from the packet.
  a foliage
  b soluble
  c abundant
  d frequency
  e seedling
  f spillage

Remember
You can use a dictionary to look up word meanings.

3 List the imperative verb in instruction 1, instruction 2 and instruction 3.

4 Identify and list an adverbial phrase from instruction 1, instruction 2 and instruction 3.

Proper nouns

The names of people, places, days, months and titles have an initial capital letter because they are **proper nouns**. Sometimes brand names on packaging, such as the name of the plant food, are written entirely in capital letters to make them stand out more.

1 Look at the back of the package on page 26.

2 List all the words and phrases that start with a capital letter except for those at the beginning of a sentence.

Plant Food
Nitrogen
Essential Trace Elements

3 Discuss with a partner why the capital letters have been used. Do you think they have used them all correctly?

Creating new proper nouns

1 This company has created the name Phostrogen by combining phosphate and nitrogen. Some people name their houses by combining their names.
Shirley and Ronald = Shirona

2 Create some new proper names by combining pairs of names in your class. Design a house plaque for the one you like best.

Words ending with vowels

English contains many words that end with a vowel. Look at all these words that end with 'o'.

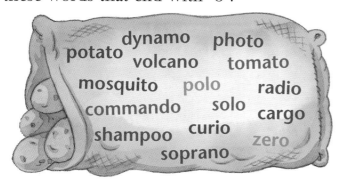

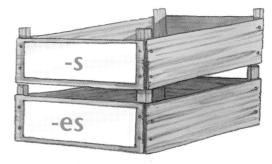

1 Decide whether you think the plural of each word in the sack needs an '-s' or an '-es'. Make two lists and put the words in the correct list. Check your answers in a dictionary.

Add '-s'
photos

Add '-es'
cargoes

2 Add as many words as you can to this list of words that end with 'a'. Work with a friend to extend your list.

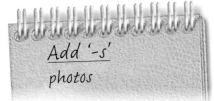

opera

zebra

idea

3 Use a dictionary to see if you can work out a rule for changing the words in your list into plurals. Do all the words in your list need changing?

4 Do the same for words that end in 'i' and words that end in 'u'.

5 Try to discover which language the words originate from by looking in an etymological dictionary. Does that help you understand the spelling rules?

Writing instructions (and more)

You have looked at instructional packaging in this unit.
Now you are going to design your own packaging which
will give instructions on how to use the contents but
will also look attractive to buy.

1 Look at the packaging you have studied in this unit
(on pages 19 and 26).

2 Brainstorm ideas for what is going to be in your Brain Food
and what it does.

Brainstorm

Plan

alphabet letters
(boosts word power)

Brain Food

3 Combine some of your ingredients to make your trade name
or play around with other ideas.

ALPHABETTER
BRAIN FOOD

4 Draft a persuasive comment for the front of the packet.

Simple to use but complex results

5 Make notes on how to use the food, quantities needed, etc.

Dissolve 1 teaspoon in ...

6 Write a first draft of the back of your packet. Do a first version (with just a rough sketch) of the front of your packet.

Draft

7 Discuss your drafts with a partner.
  a Is the back of the packet clearly set out?
  b Have you used
      headings?
      bullet points?
      lists?
      charts?
      icons?
  c Is the instruction section written in the imperative mood?
  d Are the instructions clear?
  e Is the front of the packet eye-catching and the brand name interesting?

Discuss

8 Complete a final version of your package and share it with your class.

Publish

Writing to express

In this unit you will study a poem that tells a story. This poem was written over 100 years ago but it is still exciting and interesting to read. At the end of the unit you will plan, draft and write your own ending to this story poem.

What do you notice about these words?

The Pied Piper of Hamelin

Hamelin town's in Brunswick,
By famous Hanover city;
The River Weser, deep and wide,
Washes its wall on the southern side,
A pleasanter spot you never spied;
But, when begins my ditty,
Almost five hundred years ago,
To see the townsfolk suffer so
From Vermin, was a pity.

Does this opening tell you where, when, who and what?

How many sentences are there in each verse?

Story poems

On the opposite page is the opening of the poem
'The Pied Piper of Hamelin'.

- What do you think the poem will be about?
- Where is the poem taking place?
- When is the poem taking place?
- What is the effect of the rhyme pattern?
- Who is telling the story in the poem?

What do you notice about these words?

Rats!
They fought the dogs and killed the cats,
And bit the babies in the cradles,
And ate the cheeses out of the vats,
And licked the soup from the cook's own ladles
Split open the kegs of salted sprats,
Made nests inside men's Sunday hats,
And even spoilt the women's chats
By drowning their speaking
With shrieking and squeaking
In fifty different sharps and flats.

At last the people in a body
To the town hall came flocking:
" 'Tis clear," cried they, "Our Mayor's a noddy
And as for our Corporation – shocking.
To think we buy gowns lined with ermine
For dolts who that can't or won't determine
What's best to rid us of our vermin!"

What do these phrases tell you about the rats?

What does this verse tell you about how the people were feeling?

from 'The Pied Piper of Hamelin' by Robert Browning

Understanding the poem

1 Read the start of the poem 'The Pied Piper' again.
Now answer these questions.
  a Which city is Hamelin near?
  b Why does the poet say the River Weser 'washes'
    the city walls?
  c What was causing a problem for the people?
  d How do you know the rats were inside the houses?
  e How do you know the rats were fearless of humans?
  f Why did the people go to the town hall?
  g Where do you think the money comes from to buy the
    Mayor's gown?

2 What do these words from the poem mean? If you cannot
work out the meaning look up the **definition** in a dictionary.
  a vermin   b ditty
  c vats   d kegs
  e Corporation   f ermine

3 The poem uses rhymes
at the end of lines.
Use your knowledge
of rhymes to complete
the next few lines of
the poem. The
townsfolk are talking.

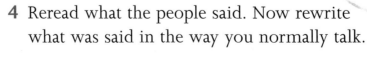

"Rouse up, sirs! Give your brains a rac[k]
To find the remedy we're _____,
Or sure as fate, we'll send you _____
At this the mayor and _____
Quaked with a mighty consternation.

4 Reread what the people said. Now rewrite
what was said in the way you normally talk.

5 Compare your version with a partner's.
How are they different from the poem?

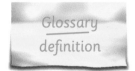

Metaphors

"At last the people in a body
To the town hall came flocking:"

This does not mean that all the people packed themselves inside one person's body. The words 'in a body' show that they were all acting together as though they were one person, not lots of people. When something is described as though it actually is something else we call this a **metaphor**.

1 Write out the metaphors in these sentences.
   a You've taken my pencil, you rat.
   b I laughed my head off at his jokes.
   c Superman is a man of steel.
   d My teacher is eagle-eyed.
   e You're an angel.

We can add other linked words and phrases to a metaphor.

EXAMPLE: The sea is a guard dog. It prowls and growls. It rushes towards me, then retreats. As I turn my back it rushes at me again and nips at my ankles.

This is called an **extended metaphor**.

2 List the opening metaphor and then all the words that add to the metaphor in this passage.

My friend Richard is an owl. He hoots with laughter when I tell a joke. At school he perches on his chair and stares unblinkingly and nods wisely so the teacher thinks he is listening. At playtime he glides to the door, then swoops on the football and carries his catch outside.

3 Select a person you know. Choose an animal or a bird, such as a cat, a hawk. Write a description of the person as though they were the animal, using an extended metaphor to help create a picture of them.

Glossary
sentence

Revising apostrophes

The poem begins by saying "Hamelin town's in Brunswick". The **apostrophe** is used to show a missing letter (an apostrophe of omission). It could be written in full as "Hamelin town is in Brunswick".

1 Write out three more examples from the poem on page 33 which use an apostrophe to show that letters have been omitted.

The poem also uses apostrophes to show who owns things. EXAMPLE: "And licked the soup from the cook's own ladles" Apostrophes that show ownership are called possessive apostrophes.

2 Write out two more examples from the poem on page 33 which use an apostrophe to show who owns things.

3 Put the missing apostrophes into the passage below. There are four missing possessive apostrophes and four missing apostrophes of omission.

Robert Browning 1812-1889

Robert Brownings poem 'The Pied Piper of Hamelin' has been popular for many years. The storys been turned into a play, a cartoon film, a musical and a pop-song. It is still printed in many childrens poetry books but it isnt always printed in full because it is a very long poem. It tells the tale of a Mayors broken promise. Because the Mayor doesnt keep his word and pay the Piper, a dreadful thing happens to the town. The poems ending is a warning that if weve promised something we should keep our word.

Antonyms

1 While the Mayor and Corporation are trying to decide what to do about the rats they hear a knock on the door. Read what happens next.

> "Come in!" – the Mayor cried, looking bigger:
> And in did come the strangest figure!
> His queer long coat from heel to head
> Was half of yellow and half of red,
> And he himself was tall and thin,
> With sharp blue eyes each like a pin,
> And light loose hair, yet swarthy skin,
> No tuft on cheek nor beard on chin
> But lips where smiles went out and in.

The poet uses words with opposite meanings (**antonyms**) to help create contrasts.
EXAMPLES: heel/head out/in

2 Write the opposite words to the words below. They are all from the extract of the poem shown above.

Come in	cried	bigger	His	he
himself	long	tall	thin	sharp
like	light	loose	smiles	

3 Now try rewriting the description of the Pied Piper using the antonyms you have chosen. You can also alter the colours if you wish.

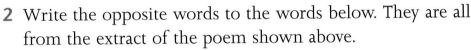

> *"Go out!" – the mayor whispered, looking ...*

4 Draw a picture to illustrate your description.

5 Compare your version with a friend's. Did you both have the same antonyms? If you have different ones talk about why this might happen.

UNIT·3 Writing to express

Grammar:
*main clauses,
subordinate
clauses, phrases*
Punctuation:
*using commas for
clauses*

Complex sentences

I am able, by using a secret charm, to draw all creatures, living beneath the sun that creep or swim or fly or run, after me!

Here is what the Piper said to the Mayor and Corporation. The Piper is using a complex sentence. Complex sentences are made up of a main clause and one or more subordinate clauses. All clauses have to contain a **verb**. A main clause can stand alone as a sentence as it makes sense on its own.

EXAMPLE: I am able to draw all creatures after me. (main clause)

A subordinate clause needs to be added to the main clause to make sense. It cannot stand on its own.

EXAMPLE: 'by using a secret charm'

1 Write out the main clause in these sentences.
   a His long coat, which covered him from heel to head, was half of yellow and half of red.
   b The Piper, who had sharp blue eyes, was tall and thin.
   c Sitting around the table, the Mayor and Corporation discussed what to do.
   d The townsfolk, wanting to complain, came to the Town Hall.
   e Using his pipe, the Piper could make creatures follow him.

Remember
If you take out a clause you take out the commas that go with it.

2 Write out these sentences. Underline the main clause in blue. Underline any subordinate clauses in red. Some of the sentences do not have subordinate clauses.
   a The Piper had long hair.
   b He carried a pipe on a string round his neck.
   c All the people noticed his clothes especially the coat he wore.
   d The people wanted to be rid of the rats which were causing great misery.
   e The rats were everywhere in the town.

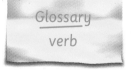

Glossary
verb

38

Punctuating complex sentences

There are three general rules for punctuating the clauses in
a complex sentence.

Rule 1
If the subordinate clause comes at the beginning of the sentence, it is separated from the main clause by a comma.
EXAMPLE: Sitting around the table, the Corporation discussed the problem.

Rule 2
If the subordinate clause splits the main clause, it is marked by commas.
EXAMPLE: The Piper, who was tall and thin, entered the room.

Rule 3
If the main clause comes first, a comma is not needed to mark the subordinate clause.
EXAMPLE: The Piper played the pipe which hung round his neck.

1 Add the missing commas to these complex sentences.
  a Jan who is tall and thin is my best friend.
  b Running quickly down the road I managed
    to catch the bus.
  c I was in the class assembly reading out my work.
  d I hope you come with us when we go to the pictures.
  e My favourite poem which I have read many times is the
    Pied Piper.

2 Add a subordinate clause to the beginning, middle or end of
  these simple sentences. Add in commas if they are needed.
  a I was late for school.
  b Rats are mammals.
  c I have a hamster.
  d Children often play the recorder.
  e I was late for school.
  f Tomorrow is my birthday.

Remember
A subordinate clause must contain a verb.

Glossary
clause
complex
    sentence
subordinate
    clause
main clause
    comma

39

More from the poem

You are now going to look closely at a further part of 'The Pied Piper of Hamelin'. The Piper has said he can get rid of the rats if the Mayor will pay him 1000 guilders. The Mayor agrees to this price.

How many sentences are there in this extract?

What does this tell you?

What do you notice about the sound intensity of these words?

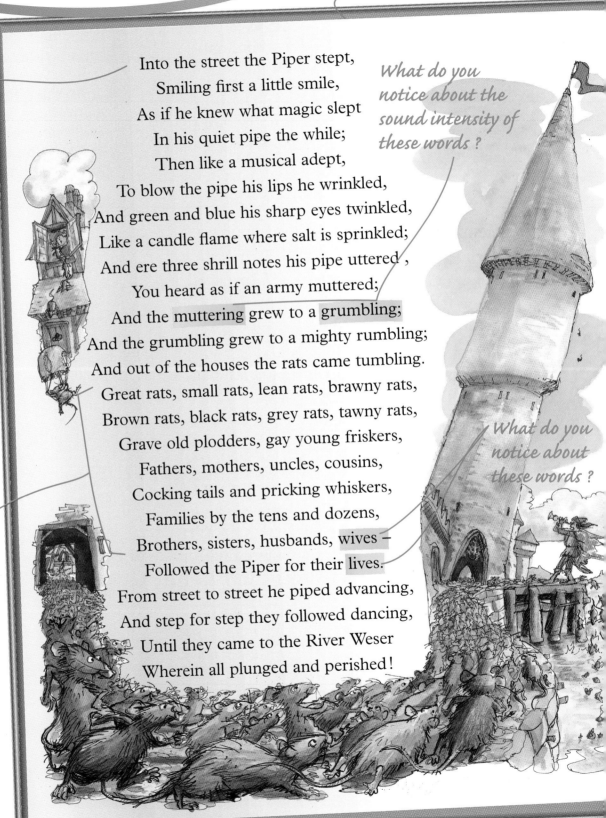

Into the street the Piper stept,
Smiling first a little smile,
As if he knew what magic slept
In his quiet pipe the while;
Then like a musical adept,
To blow the pipe his lips he wrinkled,
And green and blue his sharp eyes twinkled,
Like a candle flame where salt is sprinkled;
And ere three shrill notes his pipe uttered,
You heard as if an army muttered;
And the muttering grew to a grumbling;
And the grumbling grew to a mighty rumbling;
And out of the houses the rats came tumbling.
Great rats, small rats, lean rats, brawny rats,
Brown rats, black rats, grey rats, tawny rats,
Grave old plodders, gay young friskers,
Fathers, mothers, uncles, cousins,
Cocking tails and pricking whiskers,
Families by the tens and dozens,
Brothers, sisters, husbands, wives –
Followed the Piper for their lives.
From street to street he piped advancing,
And step for step they followed dancing,
Until they came to the River Weser
Wherein all plunged and perished!

What do these phrases tell you about the rats?

What do you notice about these words?

1 Read the poem and then answer these questions.
   a What was the Piper doing just before he began to play?
   b How many notes did he play before the rats began following him?
   c What use of words helps you know that the number of rats got greater and greater?
   d What makes you think the rats were happy to follow the Piper?
   e How did the rats die?
   f Why do you think the rats followed the Piper? What makes you think this?

2 Write an example of **alliteration** in this extract.

3 Write two examples of **antonyms** in this extract.

4 Write an example of a **simile** in this extract.

5 Practise saying this extract aloud, starting quietly and getting louder as the number of rats increases. Think about how you might say the last two lines in a different way from the other lines.

The words 'magic' and 'musical' are used in the first lines of the extract. Both of these words can be altered in the same way by adding **suffixes** to the root word.
EXAMPLES: magic   magic<u>al</u>   magi<u>cian</u>
          music   musi<u>cal</u>   musi<u>cian</u>

6 Add the suffixes '-al' and '-cian' to these words to make new words.

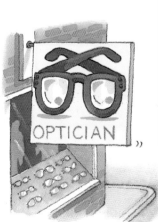

Root word	-al	-cian
technique	technical	technician
tactic		
optic		
politic		

Remember
If the word already ends in '-c' you only add '-ian'.

Glossary
alliteration
antonym
simile
suffix

7 Can you find any other examples to add to these columns?

41

Possessive pronouns

"Whose pipe is it?" she asked. "It's his," they replied. In this answer, the word 'his' tells us that the pipe belongs to the Piper. In this case 'his' is a **possessive pronoun** – it shows who the pipe belongs to.

Remember

Possessive pronouns replace the **noun**. They do not go with a noun.

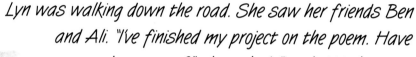

Possessive pronouns
Singular: mine, yours, his, hers, its
Plural: ours, yours, theirs

1 Read the text below and underline the possessive pronouns.

Lyn was walking down the road. She saw her friends Ben and Ali. "I've finished my project on the poem. Have you done yours?" she asked. "Yeah. We bet ours is better than yours," they teased. "No. Mine's great!" she replied. The boys waved and carried on their way. Lyn went into the park and sat down on a bench. Too late! She realized that the bench had been painted. Now her coat had stripes of red on it. "Just like the Pied Piper!" she thought. "But I bet his did not smell of paint."

2 Add the missing possessive pronouns to this passage.

When Ben and Ali got home they saw the parcel.
"It's _____ !" shouted Ben.
"No. It's _____," argued Ali.
"It's not _____ and it's not _____, said their mother.
"It's for both of you."
"OK," laughed Ben. "I agree that it's _____ if he agrees that it's _____. We'll agree that it's _____ to share. Now can we open it?"

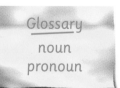

Possessive adjectives

"Whose pipe is it?" she asked. "It's his pipe."
In the answer to the question the word 'his' cannot be
a possessive pronoun because it is followed by the noun
'pipe'. 'His' is a **possessive adjective** when it is used with
a noun. It is describing the noun.

**The possessive adjectives are
Singular: my, your, his, her + noun
Plural: our, your, their + noun**

1 Look at the highlighted word in these sentences. Write
possessive adjective or possessive pronoun to show how
you think the word is being used.
 a The Mayor and Corporation were wearing their fur-
 lined gowns.
 b The man found a rat in his hat.
 c We'd like our town to be free of rats.
 d The Piper played his pipe to charm the rats.
 e Is this yours? No-one else has a red and yellow coat.
 f The women did not like the rats spoiling their chats.

Insults

When the Piper goes to collect his 1000 guilder fee, the Mayor
refuses to pay it. Instead, he insults the Piper by saying to him:
"Do your worst. Blow your pipe until you burst."

2 Invent similar insults for the people listed below. Include
a possessive adjective in each insult. The first one is done
for you.

Teacher/chalk
 a Footballer/football
 b Driver/car
 c Librarian/books
 d Singer/songs

Write with your chalk
until you wear it
down to a stump.

Writing a narrative poem

In this unit we have looked at how a story unfolds in a long narrative poem. Now you are going to write your own ending to 'The Pied Piper' before comparing it with Browning's ending.

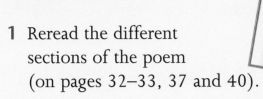

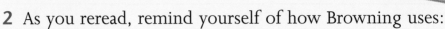

1 Reread the different sections of the poem (on pages 32–33, 37 and 40).

2 As you reread, remind yourself of how Browning uses:
- rhyme
- imagery
- opposites for contrast
- words to build up the sounds of the rats
- lists of the different types of rats to build up a picture of how many there are.

3 Reread the Mayor's insult and remember that he was also refusing to pay the Piper.

Brainstorm

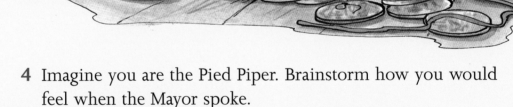

4 Imagine you are the Pied Piper. Brainstorm how you would feel when the Mayor spoke.

angry — Piper feels

5 The Piper decides to charm something else from the town. Brainstorm ideas for what he might lead away this time.

charms cattle — Piper's actions — charms pets

Plan

6 Choose one of your ideas from the web on page 44. List lots of variations of the creatures, like Browning listed lots of different rats.

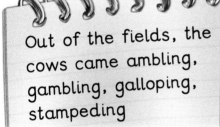

brown cows, cream cows,
calves and bullocks
beef cattle, milkers

7 Think about how they might move and where they would come from. Then play around with words that might build up a growing sound or a growing speed of movement.

Out of the fields, the
cows came ambling,
gambling, galloping,
stampeding

8 Using the section of the poem on page 40 as a model, use your ideas to write a draft verse about the Piper's revenge.

9 Swap your first draft with a partner. Get them to say which parts they think are good and why, and whether there are any parts they don't like.

10 Make any alterations that will improve your poem. Then write out your final draft and mount it.

11 Have a poetry reading session where you read your poems aloud to each other. Also read Robert Browning's ending to the poem.

Draft

Publish

45

Writing to inform

In this unit you will study reports which give information.
You will consider how to evaluate reports
and write your own.

WRITTEN COMMUNICATION

Ever since writing became widespread, people have searched for
easier, faster and less expensive ways to communicate in writing.
Today, written communication takes two main forms: writing on
paper and writing on screen.

Paper-based communication

headings to classify the main topics of the text

Letters are a traditional type
of written communication
and examples survive from
the fourteenth century.
However, it was Rowland
Hill's suggestion in 1837 that
letters should be charged by
weight and paid for by the
sender which was the basis
of the modern British postal

complex sentence

system. The Penny Black stamp,
introduced in 1840, marked the beginning
of regular use of letter post in Britain. Letter post is very
flexible. Commercial users may have franking machines which
apply postage quickly, without the need for stamps. Written
communications of all shapes and sizes can be taken to almost
anywhere in the world. However, the time letters take to arrive
has created a demand for other forms of written communication.

technical vocabulary

The facsimile (or fax machine) scans pictures and text and sends
them down a telephone line to another fax machine. The idea was
first used in the 1900s but it is in the last ten years that fax machines
have become popular.

descriptions

Text features:
*headings,
description,
passive sentences,
technical
vocabulary,
hypothetical
sentence*

Look at how this report is written.

- What does the first sentence tell you?
- What alternative headings could you suggest for this report?
- Which sentences make the passage sound impersonal?
- Where is the passage taken from?

Screen-based communication

The other important medium for written communication is electronic and does not need paper at all. Electronic mail (or e-mail) has become increasingly popular since its invention in the 1970s. Electronic mail messages can be sent from one computer to another computer or computers almost instantly, however long the communication. E-mail uses telephone lines or special cables to send messages very quickly, so reducing the cost of written communication. In businesses this means workers can send messages to other members of the same company or to people all over the world.

passive sentences to make the report less personal

Although electronic mail has become an important medium of written communication it has not replaced letters and faxes and, at the moment, is often used for less formal communications.

Who knows, the next decade may see the development of even more convenient written communication.

hypothetical sentence

47

UNIT·4 **Writing to inform**

Reading skills:
*comprehension,
dictionary use*
Words:
*technical words,
literal and
inferential
questions*

Comprehension and vocabulary

1 Reread the report about written communication on pages 46 and 47.

   a What are the two main means of written communication in the report?

   b Which type of written communication came first?

   c What were the first stamps called?

   d Which is the fastest form of written communication discussed?

   e Why do you think electronic communication has not replaced written communication using paper?

   f Why do you think some people call letters 'snail mail'?

2 Write a **definition** for each of these words.

   a popular   **b** electronic

   c facsimile   **d** scans

   e commercial   **f** franking machine

Remember

Use a dictionary and the passage on pages 46 and 47 to work out these words.

3 Complete the chart below. Remember to think about speed, cost and the equipment you need.

	Advantages	Disadvantages
Posting letters		
Sending faxes		
Using e-mail		

4 What means of written communication do you think would be best for the following situations? Say why.

   a A friend in your class communicating with a children's TV programme.

   b The headteacher communicating with your parents.

   c A child communicating with a friend.

   d A businessman communicating with a big company.

Glossary
definition

Subject and verb agreement

Most **sentences** have a **verb** and a **subject**. The subject is who or what the sentence is about.

EXAMPLES: The cat sat on the mat. **Cat** is the subject.
The computer blew up. **Computer** is the subject.

1 Write down the subject and verb in each sentence.
   a John sent a fax.
   b Asghar is feeding the duck.
   c The postwoman delivered the letter.
   d The letters will come soon.

Subjects   Verbs

The verb in a sentence must agree with the subject in tense and number.

EXAMPLES: The cat sat on the mat. **Sat** is past tense, singular.
The boys will go soon. **Will go** is future tense, plural.

2 Say whether each verb is singular or plural and whether it is past, present or future **tense**. The first one is done for you.
   a My aunties loved their birthday presents.
      Loved is plural and in the past tense.
   b Ben will be head boy this year, I think.
   c Mr Jones sent an e-mail to his cousin in Australia.
   d The girls use the fax machine too often.

Remember
Ask yourself questions about the subject of the sentence: How many? When?

3 Rewrite these sentences, making the verbs agree with the subjects.
   a The letters came through the letter box later today.
   b They send the parcel two weeks ago.
   c I ate my lunch at the moment.
   d The birds gobble up all the seeds I planted yesterday.

4 Rewrite the passage, replacing the verbs so that they agree with the subject.

Yesterday, my computer break down. It just go 'pouf' and will stop. Now I could not do anything. I needed the computer for writes letters and send e-mail. What am I do? Maybe I bought a new computer, but that was expensive!

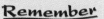

Glossary
sentence
verb
tense

Changing personal pronouns

A **pronoun** stands in for a **noun** in a **sentence**. The pronoun must agree in number (**singular** or **plural**) and gender (masculine or feminine) with the noun.

When a personal pronoun is the **subject** of a sentence we use I, you, he, she, it (**singular**) and we, you, they (**plural**).

1 Write down the missing subject pronouns.
   a My name is Jane.   come from London.
   b Sally was starving.   had not eaten breakfast.
   c My parents are late. I expect   are lost.
   d Have you been waiting long? I expect   are cold.
   e This table is useless.   too old to be safe.

Sometimes we use the personal pronouns me, you, him, her, it (singular) or we, you, them (plural). These forms are used when a personal pronoun is not the subject of a sentence, or after 'as', 'than' or the verb 'to be'.

2 Write down the missing pronouns.
   a Sally and Guy are my cousins. I like   very much.
   b He is not as tall as   .
   c Manjit has gone to America. I have written to   .
   d I didn't do it. It was   .
   e Is that you calling? Yes, it is   .

3 Rewrite the passage, putting in appropriate pronouns. The first sentence has been done for you.

Manjit and her father had a bad day.   computer broke down.   wouldn't work at all! In the end Manjit talked to a technician.   wasn't much help, but at least   knew that it could be fixed. The next day the repairman came.   mended the computer and   was business as usual.

Active and passive sentences

If the **subject** in the sentence carries out the action of the **verb** we call the **sentence active**.

EXAMPLE: The cat **sat** on the mat. (The cat did the sitting.)

If the subject of the sentence is acted upon by the verb we call the sentence **passive**.

EXAMPLE: The mat **was sat** upon by the cat.

Remember

Notice the way the verb changes in active and passive sentences.

1 Change these sentences from passive to active. The first one is done for you.

   a The computer was broken by the children.
   The children broke the computer.

   b The game was won by Chelsea.

   c The hedge was flattened by the car.

   d The tea was drunk by Mum.

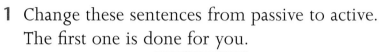

2 Now change these sentences from active to passive. The first one is done for you

   a I told the police officer about the fire.
   The police officer was told about the fire by me.

   b Ben smashed the vase.

   c My parents made a superb meal.

   d The company delivered the new computers.

Using passive sentences can make a report sound less personal. Removing the names or personal pronouns makes a sentence less personal, too.

EXAMPLE: **I have bought** a new fax machine. A new fax machine **has been bought**.

Remember

Add 'was' and 'were' and remove personal pronouns.

3 Rewrite these sentences as passive sentences without personal pronouns to make them less personal.

EXAMPLE:

The head teacher sent a fax from the new machine.
A fax was sent from the new machine.

   a She put the paper into the machine.

   b She inserted the sheet to be sent.

   c Then the headteacher pressed the button.

   d She heard a clunk from the fax machine.

   e She had broken it !

Glossary
subject
verb
sentence

Evaluating an advertisement

1 Read the following advertisement.

66 Students today can't prepare bark to calculate their problems. They depend on their slates which are more expensive. What will they do when the slate is dropped and breaks? They will be unable to write! **99**
from a teachers' conference, 1703

wrong

66 Students depend on paper too much. They don't know how to write on a slate without getting chalk dust all over themselves. They can't clean a slate properly. What will they do when they run out of paper? **99**
from a principals' publication, 1815

wrong

66 Students today depend too much upon ink. They don't know how to use a pen knife to sharpen a pencil. Pen and ink will never replace the pencil. **99**
from the National Association of Teachers (US) Journal, 1907

Wrong

66 Students today depend upon store-bought ink. They don't know how to make their own. This is a sad commentary on modern education. **99**
from Rural American Teacher, 1928

wrong

66

Smart Teachers, 2000

99

write!

Smart Teachers Inc.©

2 Answer these questions.
  a List three materials that were used for writing on in the past.
  b List three materials used to write with in the past.
  c List three reasons given for resisting changes in writing technology.
  d How does the advertisement suggest people should write now?

3 Give definitions of the following words:
   a store-bought   **b** calculate.

4 When you read a report or advertisement you should
evaluate who wrote it and why.
   a What is the advertisement aiming to sell?
   b Why do the advertisers suggest you should buy
   the product?
   c What does the advertisement suggest that people who
   don't like the product are like?

Remember
Use a dictionary
to look up words
you are unsure of.

5 Make a time line of the writing materials used by children.

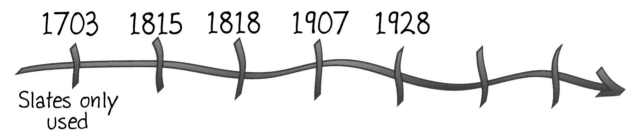

1703   1815   1818   1907   1928

Slates only
    used

6 In 1907 the teachers' association said
"Pen and ink will never replace the pencil."
Do you agree with this statement?

7 Make a chart of the advantages and disadvantages of using
word processors for writing and learning to write.

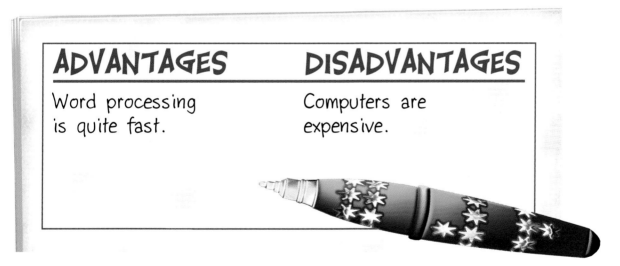

ADVANTAGES	DISADVANTAGES
Word processing is quite fast.	Computers are expensive.

8 Explain why you think that in the future word processors
will, or will not be used, for all writing.

9 List the sources of the quotations in the advertisement on
page 52.

Research skills

1 Make notes of everything Mr Jakes already knows about fax machines. Notes do not need to be in full sentences.

2 Make notes of what Mr Jakes needs to find out about fax machines.

3 List three ways Mr Jakes could find the information.

SPECIAL OFFER

9600 kbpm speed
extra fine resolution
300dpi quality – good prints
Plain paper fax – uses ordinary typing paper – no messy special rolls.
Standard size machine with large clear instructions
10 number memory
Redials automatically
Price does not include VAT

In stock now. £199

UNBEATABLE PRICE

LATEST FAX OFFER

- 9600kbpm speed
- super fine resolution
- 600DPI quality – magnificent clear faxes
- Prints onto special rolls of paper
- Convenient small size

99 number memory
Redials automatically
Orders delivered within a week.

£215 including VAT

Fax machine

Speed: 9600kbpm
Print resolution:150DPI
Paper: plain sheets
Extra features: 50 number memory, automatic redial if number engaged
Price: £200
A nifty little machine. Good performance for the price, but a bit fiddly to use. Nice quality prints. Reasonable price.
(DPI=dots per inch. kbpm=kilobytes per minute)

4 How do these advertisements catch your attention?

5 Write down all the information Mr Jakes finds out.

6 Look up the subject in an encyclopaedia or reference book. Key words you might try include fax, facsimile, electronic communication and technology.

7 Write a report to say which fax machine you think Mr Jakes should buy and why.

Hypothetical statements

"The next decade may see the development of even more convenient written communication." This is a **hypothetical** statement, because it might happen but we cannot be sure. Hypothetical statements use:

perhaps, might, could, may, it is possible that, maybe, possibly

1 Which of these are hypothetical statements?
   a The sun will rise tomorrow.
   b This price may be cheaper at another supermarket.
   c I might go to the shops later.
   d I will get the bus into town.
   e They could have a picnic on Wednesday.

2 Using words from the tinted box rewrite these statements to make them hypothetical. The first one is done for you.
   a It is going to be a lovely day.   *It might be a lovely day.*
   b Technology will change the lives of everyone on the planet.
   c The food is better at other restaurants.
   d It will rain tomorrow.
   e We can all recycle paper to save trees.

Possessive pronouns

Possessive pronouns show ownership – mine, yours, ours, theirs, his, hers, its. They replace the nouns they refer to.
EXAMPLE: That hat is **mine**. No, it is **theirs**.

1 Write out the missing possessive pronouns.
   a "Here are two bars of chocolate. The little one is ⬚⬚⬚ and the big one is ⬚⬚," said Jane, greedily.
   b That is not our cat. It is ⬚⬚ .
   c "The gold is ⬚⬚ , all ⬚⬚ ," yelled Jake. "None of it is ⬚⬚ ."
   d "Is that my coat or ⬚⬚ ?"

Glossary
statement

UNIT·4 Writing
to inform

**Writing skills,
grammar:**
*expanding and
combining
sentences*
Punctuation:
*commas in
sentences*

Expanding and combining

Before electronic communication, telegram messages were written in as few words as possible. We call this shortened text 'telegraphic'. You can use this sort of writing for making notes.

DOG ILL. COME QUICK.

I am afraid the dog is ill. Please could you come home quickly.

1 Rewrite these telegraphic messages as full sentences.
  a CAR HIT TREE.
  b TOWN HALL BURNT DOWN.
  c CAT LOST.
  d CEILING COLLAPSED.

2 Summarize these sentences in a few words.
  a Realizing I was on my own, I peeped into the biscuit tin, only to find it was empty.
  b I felt something a bit strange and realized I had lost an earring.
  c Alisdair, forgetting to put the light on, tripped over the dog and fell right on his nose.
  d I was out very late last night so now I am rather tired.

3 Rewrite these telegraphic messages using two sentences for each. EXAMPLE: Stood on rollerskate. Arm broken.
  I accidentally stood on my roller skate. I shot across the kitchen, and broke my arm at the wrist.
  a Chewed toffee. Visiting dentist.
  b Pipe burst. House flooded.
  c Missed train. Not coming today.
  e Dog fleas everywhere. Call vet.

4 Now join up the pairs of sentences to make them sound more interesting and flow better. You can change words, use commas and use **connectives** like 'because', 'so', and 'as a result'. EXAMPLE:

  I accidentally stood on one of my roller skates and shot across the kitchen, ending up with a broken arm.

Making your writing clear

From: Tom Watkins, Head teacher T.Wat@school.ac.uk

C.C. [ ]

To: Dave Clark, Chair of Governors D.Clar@school.ac.uk

B.C. [ ]

Send

Subject: Transport to school

Cancel

Message:

Dave

Important i agree. i am sure that there is too much traffic outside school. Last week watched children arriving. Saw two cars bump each other and two near misses. worried about possibility of accidents.

first need to know how many children coming to school by bus, how many by car and who is walking. Then we can say whether we need a crossing, a lollipop lady or something else.

Next step to write to all parents and explain what we need to know. Ask how their children get to school. Also for opinions about how to solve danger problems.

Print

1 Skim read the text. What is the **e-mail** message about?

2 Scan the message and pick out some details.
  Answer these questions.
  a What forms of transport to school are mentioned?
  b What solutions to the problem are mentioned?

When people send e-mail messages they often do not worry about capital letters and write in **telegraphic** form.

3 Rewrite the e-mail message as a letter adding words, punctuation and capital letters to make it clear and correct.

The School
Greenway Rd
Churston
Devon
TQ8 3BW

Dear Dave,
Thank you for your letter about the school transport situation. I agree with you that this matter is very.....

Glossary
e-mail
telegraphic text

57

Writing a report

You are going to write your own report about one of these topics:

- Transport in the area around your school
- The use of technology in your school
- Use of the playground in your school.

Discuss

1 Discuss these ideas with your partner. Select which topic you will use.

2 Make notes of what you already know about the topic. You will find discussing this with a partner may help you remember things.

3 Identify what else you could find out. Make a list of questions.

4 Decide how you are going to find more information for your report. Consider some of the following sources:
- The encyclopaedia and reference books in school
- The CD ROM and internet in school
- Interviews with other people
- Asking the opinions of your classmates by doing a survey.

5 Make notes of the information you find out.

6 Look at your plan and see how the information you have collected divides into paragraphs. Each major idea should have a paragraph of its own.

Plan

7 Write the opening paragraph of your report. It will say what the subject of the report is.

> This is a report about the transport to and from school used by members of my class. The report considers some of the difficulties children in my class encounter and suggests ...

8 Now write your report. Remember to use appropriate language so that it does not sound too personal. For example, 'This report was written' instead of 'I wrote this report'.

9 Finish your report with a hypothetical question or statement.

> If everyone at school walked instead of taking the bus, the roads might be less polluted and the children might be healthier.

10 Swap your first draft with a friend. Get them to say which parts they think are good and how you could improve your report.

11 Make any changes that will improve your report. Then check the capital letters, full stops and question marks.

12 Think about how you are going to illustrate your report. Does it need a diagram?

13 Complete your final version.

Draft

Revise

Publish

Writing to entertain

In this unit you will study stories from another continent – Africa.
At the end of the unit you will plan, draft and write your own story.

plot suggested at the beginning

clue to the story

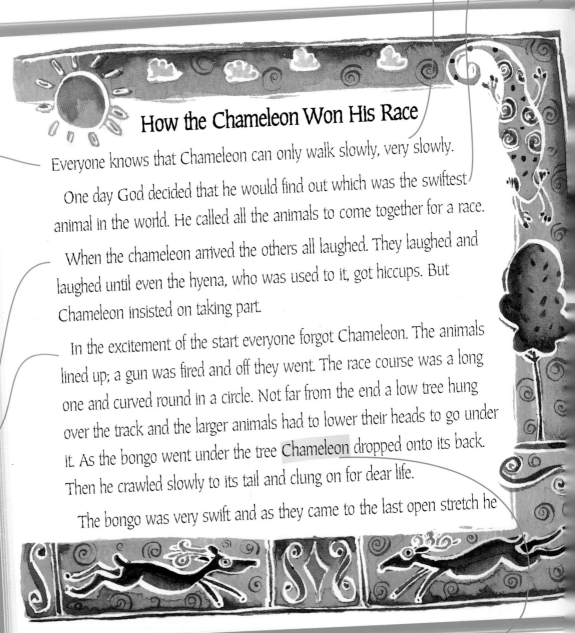

How the Chameleon Won His Race

opening words include the reader as part of the group

Everyone knows that Chameleon can only walk slowly, very slowly.

One day God decided that he would find out which was the swiftest animal in the world. He called all the animals to come together for a race.

When the chameleon arrived the others all laughed. They laughed and laughed until even the hyena, who was used to it, got hiccups. But Chameleon insisted on taking part.

action of the story divided into paragraphs

In the excitement of the start everyone forgot Chameleon. The animals lined up; a gun was fired and off they went. The race course was a long one and curved round in a circle. Not far from the end a low tree hung over the track and the larger animals had to lower their heads to go under it. As the bongo went under the tree Chameleon dropped onto its back. Then he crawled slowly to its tail and clung on for dear life.

The bongo was very swift and as they came to the last open stretch he

main character

A story from the Ashanti, Ghana

- Why did the Ashanti people tell this story?
- Does it remind you of any other stories?
- Do you know other stories where the animals can talk?
- Why do you think 'talking' animals are a common story device?

drew ahead of the other animals. At the end of the course a large stool had been placed and the winning animal had to sit on it.

The bongo reached the stool and was about to sit when he heard a small voice.

"Hi, Brother Bongo, do you want to sit on me?"

Bongo turned round and looked. There sat Chameleon, who had, of course, dropped off his tail.

"How on earth did you get there, Brother Chameleon?" he asked in amazement. "There was no one ahead of me."

"I'm rather small and you just did not see me," replied Chameleon.

Chameleon was, of course, declared victor. They all knew he could not have won the race by his swiftness, but they could prove nothing. Perhaps that is why some people think the chameleon has magic powers. What do you think?

some of the story told through dialogue

direct remark addressed to the reader

conclusion

from *Why the Hyena does not care for Fish and Other Tales from the Ashanti* by Peggy Appiah

UNIT·5 Writing to entertain

Reading skills:
comprehension
Vocabulary:
*definitions,
writing: different
viewpoints*

Understanding the story

1 Reread the story on pages 60 and 61 and then answer these questions.

   a What did God want to find out?

   b How was he going to find the answer?

   c Why did all the animals laugh?

   d What does it mean when it says the hyena was 'used to it'?

   e How did the chameleon get on to the bongo's tail?

   f Why do you think the other animals did not see the chameleon on the bongo's tail?

   g What characteristic of the chameleon, which is not directly mentioned in the story, might make people think he had magic powers?

2 Find these words in the story and give a **definition** for each one.

   a swiftest

   b hiccups

   c insisted

   d amazement

   e victor

Remember
You can use
a dictionary
to check your
definition.

The story is told by a storyteller. It would be told in a different way if it were told by the chameleon or by the bongo.

3 Rewrite the story as the chameleon might tell it.

I know I move slowly but when I heard there was going to be a race I decided to take part anyway ...

Using dialogue to tell the story

Text features:
using dialogue
Grammar:
*adverbs,
punctuating,
dialogue*

Part of the chameleon story is told through the speech of
the bongo and the chameleon. The **direct speech** tells us
how the characters think, feel and act.

1   Here are some comments which could be used in the story.
Add **verbs** and **adverbs** to show how the speaker is feeling.
The first one is done for you.

  a   "Look, Chameleon is coming to join the race," giggled
the giraffe gaily.

  b   "You've no chance of winning," the hyena ▢▢▢ .

  c   "I'll show you I can win," ▢▢ the chameleon ▢ .

  d   The bongo ▢▢▢ , "I'm ahead of all the
other animals."

  e   The animals ▢▢ , "Chameleon must have
magic powers."

2   The word 'giggled' is a **synonym** for 'laughed'. How many
other synonyms can you add?

<u>Laugh</u>
giggle
chuckle

The words the animals speak are shown by **speech marks**.
If the actual words spoken are interrupted by any other
words such as 'he said' the speech marks have to start
again when the words start again.

EXAMPLE: "Can I join the race?" he asked. "I like races."

Remember
Punctuation such
as full stops,
capital letters,
commas, etc.
go inside the
speech marks.

3   Copy this passage putting in the missing speech marks.

I don't understand how Chameleon won, puzzled the bongo. He walks so
slowly. I know I run faster than him. How did he get to the chair first?

He must have cheated, agreed the leopard. But I don't know how.

Do you think he used magic? asked the hyena. Nobody saw him.

Don't be silly, said the zebra scornfully. It was a trick, not magic.

Glossary
direct speech
verbs
adverbs
synonym
speech marks

Changing the meaning of words

The animals found it unbelievable and incredible that the chameleon won the race. It was improbable that he could run fast enough. They wondered if the chameleon had done something illegal in order to win.

The **prefixes** 'un-', 'im-', 'in-' and 'il-' often mean 'not'. Adding them to a base word changes the meaning of the base word into a negative meaning.

1 Add 'un-', 'im-', 'in-' or 'il-' to these words to change their meaning. The first one is done for you. Then add any more words you can think of that belong in the box.

'un-'		'in-'	
- done	*undone*	-sane	
- known		-audible	
- opposed			
'il-'		'im-'	
- literate		-possible	
- legible		-perfect	
- logical			

2 Choose four of the words you have created – one beginning with each prefix. Use each word in a sentence to show what the word means.

SALE
Slightly imperfect, half price

3 Rewrite these sentences replacing the negative phrase with one word.
  a There is only one not eaten chocolate left in the box.
  b She was not able to sing the song.
  c It is not likely that we will go out tonight.
  d He shouted for help but his cries were not heard.
  e The mouldy jam was not edible.

Joining sentences

Here is a passage from the chameleon story you read on pages 60–61.

The animals lined up; a gun was fired and off they went. The race course was a long one and curved round in a circle. Not far from the end a low tree hung over the track and the larger animals had to lower their heads to go under it. As the bongo went under the tree Chameleon dropped on to its back. Then he crawled slowly to its tail and clung on for dear life.

    The bongo was very swift and as they came to the last open stretch he drew ahead of the other animals. At the end of the course a large stool had been placed and the winning animal had to sit on it.

1 Read the passage and count how many times the author uses the **conjunction** 'and' to join two **sentences** together.

It can be boring to use the same conjunction too many times. Each time 'and' is used in the passage above the sentence could be rewritten to use a different conjunction.
EXAMPLE: A gun was fired and off they went.
When a gun was fired, off they went.

2 Here are some conjunctions.

since   yet   which

where whilst because if

through

so   as   although or

unless then while when

but and

3 Rewrite the passage above so that you do not use 'and' to link sentences. Use a different conjunction each time.

4 Choose four conjunctions from the conjunctions given above. Use each one to link two sentences that describe an animal.
EXAMPLE: <u>Although</u> the cat is a domestic pet it is still a fierce hunter.

Remember
A conjunction can come at the beginning of a sentence as well as in the middle.

Glossary
conjunction
sentence

Proverbs

Here is another Ashanti story.

How the Deer Lost its Long Horns

Once the deer had such long and strong horns that it was feared by all the other animals. It was always wounding them accidentally. So they got together to discuss how to protect themselves.

The deer was as anxious as they were to be at peace. Together they decided that the best thing would be to push the horns down a little.

The animals pushed and pushed and pushed.

They pushed so hard the horns nearly disappeared.

When the deer realized how necessary the horns had been for his defence, it was, alas, too late. From that time to this he has been forced to rely on his swiftness to escape from trouble.

Thus the Elders say: "Had I known is always too late." "*Nim-saa ka akyire.*"

We call this kind of 'rule' at the end of a story a 'moral' or a 'proverb'. These are sayings that can be applied to other situations, not just the story that has been told.

1 Here are some proverbs. Say what you think each one means.

"It's no good crying over spilt milk" means …

"Too many cooks spoil the broth" means …

"Half a loaf is better than none" means …

We could make up-to-date versions of proverbs.
EXAMPLE: "Too many cooks spoil the broth" becomes "Too many hands on the keyboard spoil the story-writing'.

2 Make up modern versions for the other proverbs in question 1.

3 Make up a proverb for your classroom.
EXAMPLE: *"A rainy day makes tempers fray."*

Revising apostrophes

Most **plural** words end in 's', but not all.

1 Make these words plurals and sort them into three groups.

deer   dog   cat   sheep   leopard

mouse   giraffe   goose   salmon   fox

Adds 's' to become plural

Changes the word to become plural

Stays the same for singular and plural

For most words, to show **singular** possession we add an **apostrophe** followed by an 's'. For the plural we add an apostrophe after the 's'.

EXAMPLE: the dog's tail (one dog)

the dogs' tails (more than one dog)

2 Add the apostrophe to these sentences.

  a   The Elders stories often have a moral.

  b   The giraffes neck is very long.

  c   The leopards spots are brown and black.

If the words change in the plural, we add an apostrophe followed by 's' to the singular and plural forms.

EXAMPLE: the mouse's tail (one mouse)

the mice's tails (more than one)

3 Add the apostrophe to these sentences.

  a   A gooses feathers are white.

  b   Geeses bills are orange.

  c   The oxs tail flicked.

  d   The oxens heads were lowered.

4 Write out the apostrophe rule for words that stay the same in the singular and the plural.

Apostrophe Rule
For the word that stays the same...

Glossary

plural
singular
apostrophe

5 Make up three sentences to show how your rule works.

Another Ashanti story

You are now going to look at a further Ashanti story. This story explains how an animal got its distinguishing features. Many cultures tell stories explaining how living things were created and why they look as they do.

Why the Leopard Has Spots

opening paragraph gives who? what? where? and when?

All the animals were going to a funeral. As they went they passed by a garden-egg farm, full of wonderful, ripe garden eggs. Now the leopard had a passion for garden eggs. He slipped from the path and started to eat. He ate and he ate until half of the crop was consumed. Then he rejoined the path and went on his way.

main character

Soon after, the farmer reached his farm. When he saw what had happened he ran after the animals, cursing and swearing and accusing them of stealing his crop. This all the animals denied warmly.

"Will you prove it?" asked the farmer.

"How?" asked the animals.

some of the story told through dialogue

"I will build a fire and you will all jump over it. He who falls into the flames will be the thief."

action of the story divided into paragraphs

The animals agreed and the leopard smiled to himself. It was not possible that he, the great leopard, could fall in the fire. One by one the animals jumped. Even the little mouse managed somehow. When it came to the leopard's turn, he ran to the fire; he got ready to spring; he leapt into the air – but he forgot the garden eggs which lay heavy in his stomach. Instead of coming down on the other side of the fire he fell short and rolled in the embers. He howled and rushed from the fire, but not soon enough. The fire had burnt patches on his fur, some brown, some black.

conclusion

The animals stared in amazement and then started to hoot and cry out "Thief, thief." He turned tail and ran. And so from that day to this the leopard carries a spotted coat in memory of his greed.

UNIT·5 **Writing
to entertain**

Text features:
*characters, setting,
plot*
Vocabulary:
clichés

1 Read the story and then answer these questions.
   a Why did the leopard go into the farm?
   b Why did the farmer run after the animals?
   c What test did the farmer set for the animals?
   d Why did the leopard think it was an easy test?
   e Why did the leopard fall in the fire?
   f How did the leopard get the spots on his fur?
   g What is the leopard's punishment for his greed?

2 What do these words from the story mean? If you cannot
   work out the meaning look up the definition in a dictionary.
   a cursing
   b warmly
   c embers
   d greed

The final sentence of the story contains the phrase 'from that
day to this'. Some phrases get used a lot to start and end stories.
If they get used too often they become **clichés** – over-used and
predictable phrases.

3 Make a list of all the clichéd story beginnings and endings
   you can think of.

   Once upon a time ...
   Then I woke up and it was all a dream ...

4 Make up an alternative for the 'from that day to
   this' sentence.
   EXAMPLE: *Millions of minutes have past since that shameful
   leap but the leopard still carries a spotted coat.*

Glossary

cliché

69

Punctuating complex sentences

In Unit 3 you looked at some general rules for punctuating **complex** sentences. Here are the three rules again, to remind you.

Rule 1
If the **subordinate clause** comes at the beginning of the sentence, it is separated from the **main clause** by a comma.
EXAMPLE: Cursing and swearing, the farmer ran after the animals.

Rule 2
If the subordinate clause splits the main clause, it is marked by commas.
EXAMPLE: It was not possible that he, the great leopard, could fall in the fire.

Rule 3
If the main clause comes first, a comma is not needed to mark the surbordinate clause.
EXAMPLE: He ate and ate until half the crop was consumed.

1 Here are some **main clauses**. Think of a **subordinate clause** to add to each main clause, and put in the correct punctuation. Try to put the subordinate clauses in different positions within the **sentence**. The first one is done for you.

a The farm had a crop of garden eggs.

The farm, which was near the path, had a crop of garden eggs.

b The leopard crept into the farm.
c The farmer was very angry.
d The animals denied eating the crop.
e The farmer suggested a test.
f The little mouse jumped over the fire.
g The leopard ran towards the fire.
h The leopard fell in the flames.
i Leopards have brown and black spots.
j The leopard deserved his punishment.
k I felt sorry for the farmer.

Glossary

complex
clause
main clause
sentence
subordinate

2 Write 3 complex sentences describing your classroom.

Prepositions

In the leopard story the farmer says, "I will build a fire and you will all jump over it." The word 'over' is a **preposition** – a word that indicates position. Here are some common prepositions.

in on above next around to alongside over under into between by below down behind through in front of away from

1   Find the four prepositions or prepositional phrases in the opening paragraph of the story 'Why the Leopard Has Spots'.

> All the animals were going to a funeral. As they went they passed by a garden-egg farm, full of wonderful, ripe garden eggs. Now the leopard had a passion for garden eggs. He slipped from the path and started to eat. He ate and he ate until half of the crop was consumed. Then he rejoined the path and went on his way.

2   Rewrite the passage substituting a new preposition or prepositional phrase for the ones you have found. It has been started for you.

   All the animals were going away from a funeral ...

3   Compare your version with a partner's. How do they vary? What difference does changing the prepositions make to the passage?

> **Remember**
> Check in a dictionary if you are not sure of the meaning of a word.

4   These pictograms illustrate meanings of some prepositions. Select 2 or 3 prepositions and draw pictograms to illustrate their meaning.

Writing a short story

You have looked at several short stories in this unit. They are all based on explaining or using distinctive animal characteristics. Now you are going to write your own story explaining how an animal came to look as it does.

1 Reread the different stories in the unit.
As you read, remind yourself of how
- the opening of the stories introduces:
  - characters
  - setting
  - clues to the plot
- the middle of the stories:
  - sets up a problem
  - has actions to try to solve the problem
- the end of the stories:
  - shows the consequences of the actions
  - might comment on the action or draw a moral.

2 Brainstorm four or five animals that have a distinctive characteristic.

sheepdog

animals

curly tail

pig

long, shaggy coat

Brainstorm

3 Choose one of your ideas. Think of some funny reasons to explain why the animal has this characteristic.

Long, shaggy coat –
- got covered in glue and then rolled in haystack
- missed paying the animal barber who then refused to cut the dog's hair ever again
- used to have tight curly hair but had a fright and it uncurled and has been straight ever since

72

4 Make a plan to show the main introduction, events and conclusion of the story.

introduction 〜〜➤ events 〜〜➤ conclusion

Plan

5 Add details about the characters, setting and events to your plan. If you are going to have a moral add a final line.

Moral: Always pay your barber.

6 Now use your full plan to write a draft of the story. Put in plenty of details so that the reader will find your story interesting and easy to understand.

7 Swap your draft with a friend. Discuss these questions.
- Is the story easy to understand?
- Are the characters and setting easy to imagine?
- Is the story plausible? Does it give a good explanation of the characteristic?
- Is there any way the story could be better?

Draft

8 Talk about these questions with your partner and mark any changes you want to make on the draft. Check any spellings you are not sure about.

Discuss

9 Write out your story. Make a class display or class book.

YEAR 5's Animal Stories

Publish

Glossary

adjective   A word that goes with a noun and tells us about it. EXAMPLE: a blue balloon. A comparative adjective can be used to compare nouns. EXAMPLE: The boy was bigger than his friend. A superlative adjective can be used to compare something with all the others. EXAMPLE: The boy was the biggest in the class. A possessive adjective describes who the noun belongs to: Mine, his, her, your, their

adverb   A word that tells us about a verb. Some adverbs have the suffix -ly. EXAMPLES: happily, merrily
Common types of adjectives include adverbs of:

Degree	adverbs which modify another adverb: more, very
Manner	softly, happily
Time	soon, now
Place	here, there

agreement   In sentences some words or phrases are linked in meaning. This means they agree in terms of:

Tense	yesterday we went out
Number	the dogs ate their dinner
Gender	the girl picked up her coat
Person	I want my mum!

alliteration   A number of words close together which begin with a similar consonant sound. EXAMPLES: ten tired teddies, sliding slithery snakes

antonym   A word with a meaning opposite to another. EXAMPLE: hot and cold.

apostrophe   An apostrophe is a mark used to show that a letter has been left out. EXAMPLE: he is can be written as he's
Apostrophes are also used to show ownership.
EXAMPLE: the cat's bowl

argument   A written argument makes a point and gives evidence to support it.

auxiliary verb   See verb. Usually the verbs to be, to have or to do.

bullet point   A bullet point is a punctuation mark emphasising items in a list.

category word   A category word describes a set of items. EXAMPLE: the category word footwear includes shoes, slippers, socks etc.

cast list   A list of characters in a play, usually place at the start of a playscript.

character   A character is an individual in a story, play or poem.

clause   A distinct part of a sentence including a verb. A main clause makes sense on its own. A subordinate clause adds detail to the main clause but does not make sense on its own.
EXAMPLE: Although it was foggy, I went out.
            (subordinate clause) (main clause)

colon   A puctuation mark to introduce a list.

comma	A punctuation mark used to break up sentences so that they are easier to understand. Commas are used to separate items in a list that are part of a sentence. EXAMPLE: I bought eggs, fish and some chocolate. Commas are also used to separate clauses. EXAMPLE: Although she is old, the cat is beautiful. Commas can be used for parenthesis (embedding extra information in a sentence) EXAMPLE: The cat, which was very old, was sitting on the mat.
command	A type of sentence that tells someone what to do.
compound word	A word made from two other words. EXAMPLE: footpath.
common gender words	A word which can refer to men, women or both. EXAMPLE: passenger, doctor.
cliché	A phrase or expression which, through over-use, has lost its impact.
connective	A word or group of words which links sentences or parts of sentences. EXAMPLES: and, then, but, even, so.
conjunction	A conjunction is a word used to join sentences or parts of sentences. EXAMPLE: and, but, then, because
definition	A statement giving the meaning of a word or phrase.
description	Words which enable the reader/listener to form an idea of an object, event or feeling.
dialogue	Speech between two or more people.
direct speech	Speech written exactly as it is said. In books this is usually in speech marks. In a playscript direct speech is not placed in speech marks.
draft	A piece of writing which is not in finished form.
edit	To change the grammar, spelling, punctuation or words in writing.
e-mail	A message sent electronically. Less formal than a written letter.
exclamation	A type of sentence that expresses feeling. Exclamations end with an exclamation mark. EXAMPLE: Help me, please! One of four sentence types (question, statement and command are the others).
exclamation mark	A punctuation mark used at the end of a sentence to indicate strong feelings. EXAMPLE: Help!
first person	The first person pronoun is I. In writing it is used when the writer is writing about him or herself.
formal language/ informal language	Formal language is the speech and writing we use for people we do not know well. EXAMPLE: How do you do? Informal language is the language we use for people we know well. EXAMPLE: Hi!
full stop	A full stop is a mark used to end a sentence when the sentence is not a question or exclamation. EXAMPLE: The cat sat on the mat.
gender words (masculine and feminine)	Gender words tell you about the sex of the person or animal. They can only apply to either men or women, not both. EXAMPLE: prince (masculine gender), princess (feminine gender)
homonym	Words with the same form but different meanings. EXAMPLE: Tom saw a lion. Gill uses a saw to cut wood.
homophone	Words with the same sound but different meanings.

introduction	The beginning of a piece of writing.
imperative	An imperative word commands or tells the reader or listener to do something. EXAMPLE: Run over there.
label	The words which tell us about part of a diagram, picture or map.
language	Language is what people use to share their thoughts with each other. We talk with our voices. This is spoken language. When we write we use written language.
main clause	See clause
narrator	The person whose voice is heard in a novel or story. The narrator can be one of the characters speaking (first person) or someone speaking about the characters (third person). In a play the narrator may speak about what is happening to the characters on stage.
noun	A word that names a person, feeling or thing.
novel	A long story which deals with issues wider than the storyline alone.
parenthesis	Embedding extra information in a sentence using commas, dashes or brackets. EXAMPLE: The cat, which was very old, was sitting on the mat. The cat – which was very old – was sitting on the mat. The cat (which was very old) was sitting on the mat
persuade	To persuade is to try to make or convince someone to do something.
plan	Notes used to start a piece of writing.
playscript	Format in which a play is written. A playscript displays dialogue clearly.
plot	The plan or essential facts of a story.
plural	More than one.
prefix	A unit of meaning (morpheme) added to the beginning of a word to change its meaning. EXAMPLE: un-do, im-proper.
preposition	A word telling us about the place of nouns or pronouns. EXAMPLES: on, under, in
pronoun	A word used instead of a noun or noun phrase to avoid repetition in a sentence. EXAMPLE: The cat was old but she was sprightly. Personal pronouns: I, me, we, us, you, they, them Possessive pronouns: my, your, their, his, hers
proper noun	Words that name particular people, things or feelings. Proper nouns begin with capital letters. EXAMPLES: Christmas, London, Jamilla
question	A sentence which needs a response. It ends with a question mark. One of four sentence types (exclamation, statement and command are the others)
question mark	The punctuation mark at the end of a question.
regular/ irregular verb	Verbs which form the past tense by adding -ed are regular. Others do not add -ed. They are irregular verbs.
recount	A text which retells events for entertainment and/or information. Written or told in the past tense.
reported speech	A report of what has been said, but not in the exact words of the speaker.

revise	To make changes to a piece of writing to improve it.
sentence	A unit of written language which makes sense on its own (commands, questions, exclamations and statements are four sentence types). Simple sentences have one clause. EXAMPLE: The cat sat on the mat. Complex sentences have a main clause and a subordinate clause. EXAMPLE: The cat sat, licking its paws, on the mat. Compound sentences have two clauses joined by a conjunction. EXAMPLE: The cat sat and chewed its tail.
setting	The time and place of events in a story.
simile	A sentence or group of words which compares something to something else. EXAMPLE: He was as free as a bird.
singular	One of something.
speech marks	The inverted commas that go around what is actually said in direct speech. EXAMPLE: "I want my teddy," said the little boy.
stage directions	Words, phrases or sentences in a playscript which tell actors how to behave or speak.
statement	A type of sentence which tells us something. EXAMPLE: I am called Jane. One of four sentence types (question, exclamation and command are the others)
subject	The 'who' or 'what' a sentence is about. The word or phrase the verb relates to. EXAMPLES: The cat sat on the mat. Mum left her bag.
subordinate clause	See clause.
suffixes	Endings that are added to words. A suffix can change words from singular to plural (EXAMPLE: box/box**es**); can change the tense of a verb (EXAMPLE: jump /jump**ed**) or can change the function of a word (EXAMPLE: teach/teach**er**).
synonym	Words which have the same or very close meanings. EXAMPLE: big, large, huge.
telegraphic text	A text reduced to the fewest possible elements of meaning.
tense, past tense, present tense, future tense	Tense tells us when something is happening. Past tense. Something has already happened. EXAMPLE: I **sat** down. I **was sitting** down. Present tense. Something is happening now. EXAMPLE: She **is sitting** down. She **sits** down. Future tense. Something which will happen. EXAMPLE: She **will sit** down.
time line	A device for organising events in chronological order.
title	The heading which tells us what writing is about.
verb	A verb is a word or phrase that tells us what people are doing or being. EXAMPLE: The girls **ran** away. A verb phrase may have a main verb and auxiliary verbs. EXAMPLE: The car **can be** washed after the trip. Can and be are auxiliary verbs. Washed is the main verb.
vocabulary	Our vocabulary is the words we know and use.
word	A word is a group of sounds or letters that have meaning. Written words have spaces at each side. EXAMPLE: My name is Jane. This sentence contains four words.

OXFORD
UNIVERSITY PRESS

Great Clarendon Street, Oxford, OX2 6DP

Oxford University Press is a department of the University of Oxford and furthers the University's aim of excellence in research, scholarship, and education by publishing worldwide in

Oxford New York

Athens Auckland Bangkok Bogotá Buenos Aires Cape Town Chennai Dar es Salaam Delhi Florence Hong Kong Istanbul Karachi Kolkata Kuala Lumpur Madrid Melbourne Mexico City Mumbai Nairobi Paris São Paolo Shanghai Singapore Taipei Tokyo Toronto Warsaw

and associated companies in Berlin Ibadan

Oxford is a registered trade mark of Oxford University Press

British Library Cataloguing in Publication Data

Data available

Illustrated by: Kate Davies, Val Hill, Alan Marks, Bethan Matthews, Uwe Mayer, Shelagh McNicholas, Patricia Moffett, Jill Newton, Wendy Sinclair and Mike Spoor

Photographs by: Telegraph Colour Library-Abraham Menashe (p24), Corbis (p36), Mark Mason (p46).

Cover photograph by: Stock File

Acknowledgements
We are grateful to the following for permission to reproduce copyright material in this book:
David Higham Associates for extracts from Roald Dahl: *Charlie and the Chocolate Factory* (Viking, 1995) text copyright © Roald Dahl Nominee Ltd 1964, and from play edition, (Puffin, 1979), copyright © Roald Dahl and Richard R George 1964; The C S Lewis Estate c/o Adley Consulting for C S Lewis: *The Lion, The Witch and the Wardrobe* in the stage adaptation by Adrian Mitchell; The Peters Fraser and Dunlop Group on behalf of Adrian Mitchell for stage adaptation of C S Lewis: *The Lion, The Witch and the Wardrobe*, Act 1 Scenes 2 and 3 (Oberon Books), copyright © adaptation and lyrics by Adrian Mitchell. Educational Health Warning! Adrian Mitchell asks that none of his works are used in conjunction with any examinations whatsoever; Phostrogen Ltd for Phostrogen Plant Food packaging and Phostrogen logo; The Publishing and Licensing Company at Merseyside Television for extract from Phil Redmond's playscript for 'Foster', *Grange Hill* (Longman, 1985), copyright © Phil Redmond 1977; Scholastic Ltd for three tales from Peggy Appiah: *Why the Hyena Does Not Care for Fish and Other Tales from the Ashanti* (Andre Deutsch, 1977), text copyright ©1977 by Peggy Appiah; Suttons for Suttons Seed packaging for ornamental gourds.

ISBN 0 19 915552 6

Printed in China